"Pastor Landrum's book
power and life of Luther
great theological insight,
better preachers. That is what Luther wanted, and what you will
gain from Landrum's treatment of the most important matter in
all of theology and life: what God is doing with us sinners beyond
the law."

—STEVEN PAULSON, Senior Fellow, 1517.org

"Written from the perspective of pastoral care, Dr. Landrum
has provided an important survey of the academic conversation
concerning Luther's understanding of the hidden God. The book
serves to make deep theological conversation amongst Lutheran
theologians accessible while at the same time showing the way
in which an evangelical understanding of Luther's hidden God
furthers the proclamation of Christ in the world."

—CHRISTOPHER M. CROGHAN, Codirector,
the Luther House of Study

"Dr. Landrum's book is a welcome addition to a growing body
of literature on Luther and the hidden God. It provides a clean
overview of traditional and contemporary discussions of Luther's
Deus absconditus while moving the conversation away from theoretical concerns to practical. In this way, Dr. Landrum captures
the spirit of Martin Luther in putting theology into practice for
the sake of fallen souls."

—DANIEL DEEN, Concordia University Irvine

"Dr. Landrum's commitment to both Lutheran doctrine and pastoral ministry is made evident in this work. His thorough study
of Luther's understanding of the problem of evil and divine hiddenness . . . is a significant contribution to understanding of the
historical and theological discussion of the topic. Additionally,

he develops his own apologetic based on Luther's thought to help those who need to be comforted by the proclamation of the gospel."

—Mark Gstohl, Xavier University of Louisiana

"The thoughtful Christian cannot sweep the problem of divine hiddenness under the rug. It is a theological challenge of the highest order, one that must be confronted with courage. Landrum's work skillfully proposes a way forward that is unapologetically apologetic and elevates the conversation in new ways that I find quite useful. For those who are inclined to explore the sometimes-unsettling depths of a proper *theologia crucis*, this text is an excellent entry point."

—Joel Oesch, Concordia University Irvine

Martin Luther's Hidden God

Martin Luther's Hidden God

Toward a Lutheran Apologetic
for the Problem of Evil and Divine Hiddenness

TIMOTHY SCOTT LANDRUM

Foreword by STEVEN D. PAULSON

WIPF & STOCK · Eugene, Oregon

MARTIN LUTHER'S HIDDEN GOD
Toward a Lutheran Apologetic for the Problem of Evil and Divine Hiddenness

Wipf & Stock
An Imprint of Wipf and Stock Publishers
199 W. 8th Ave., Suite 3
Eugene, OR 97401

www.wipfandstock.com

PAPERBACK ISBN: 978-1-6667-1849-2
HARDCOVER ISBN: 978-1-6667-1850-8
EBOOK ISBN: 978-1-6667-1851-5

To my mother, Ann, and my wife, Susan

Contents

Foreword

PREACHERS, MINISTERS, PRIESTS, OR pastors (what Peter calls the "royal priesthood" in 1 Pet 2:9) are on the frontline of the war with evil. These Christians are usually the first responders, and often the only care-givers who show up for sickness, death, disaster, hatred, lying, cheating, coveting, and the like. Consequently, they are often the first victims in this panoply of human ills. As Solomon said, that is why a preacher needs to know the time to live and the time to die—the time to seek and the time to lose (see Eccl 3:2–8). Preachers themselves should know, then, what weapons they have in entering this fight, and what cures or remedies they supply. Their hearers should also know about these weapons and instruments, so that their own suffering dares to call upon their preacher in their own trials. God's standard instrument for fighting evil is not one of the world's usual suspects (intellect or will). Instead, it is a distinction between two words with their two kinds of cures: one that threatens, and one that comforts. When used as God intended—that is, by preaching—both are divine. They really work. When used poorly, aside from the Holy Spirit, only one of the words works, and that in a ragged, brutal, and often protracted way.

That is why I am especially pleased to have an outstanding practitioner of the holy gospel writing this book—a real preacher. Pastor Landrum is the best kind of man to explain the greatest of all theological distinctions: that between God preached and unpreached. The difference is not that with God unpreached, you get no God, but that you truly get no faith. You will get God in this world, like it or not. But you are not the source of your own comfort in evil. You cannot bleed blood from a turnip, and you cannot squeeze faith out of an unpreached God. He will not have it. What you need in your time of trouble is a true, actual, real preacher. Without it, you really will conclude with Solomon: "Vanity of vanities . . . ! All is vanity" (Eccl 1:2 ESV). That is not claiming that God doesn't exist or that evil is not real. It means that an unpreached God never does anything but threaten and terrorize. There is no cure and not even a little salve for this. But a person who gets a real preacher—that is, one who gives him the divine word of promise—is not just told why there is evil by way of some bloated explanation but actually has the evil defeated. God preached does not mean "God-splaining" things—it is at work conquering, defeating, and destroying the evil once and for all. If this is unusual language for you, then this book will correct that lack. If I were a preacher, I would want to know what God preached and unpreached means. Even if I were a hearer of preachers, I would likewise want to learn these things, since this is the only cure for what happens to all of us "under the sun" (Eccl 1:14).

But we can face facts, as theologians of the cross always must. Most people know nothing about preachers. Those that do, usually despise them. Instead, people look for another source for care in times of trouble other than hapless preachers. What we intellectuals think of as the lower type of people look for a substance to take care of them—typically, alcohol—which remedy has been tested ad nauseam. Alcohol and related chemicals have never worked for facing evil, but after all this failure, they retain an aura of "possibility" when one is in the trial. It feels to many like it just may work for them, even though it has never worked for anyone else. The higher type of thinkers look not for a lowly substance but for a lofty *idea*. Yet, this search has also failed repeatedly. Indeed, there has been an impressive array of attempts that has now come to be called "philosophy" (though philosophers rarely admit that this is what they are).

What are people doing who try to think their way out of trouble in life? Thinking anything at all (philosophy) starts not with "first principles," like mathematics, but with evil. Normally, such thinkers get evil in the mind, because they themselves have fallen into it or are at least observing someone near to them suffer it. Thinking thus belongs less to mathematics and more to therapy. After all, evil is not in need of a first principle but a cure. The cure appears to hide in the specific question of why: "Why is there evil?" The place the mind goes to gain the answer to that most basic question in life is the very beginning of "thinking," but it is also the beginning of refusing to listen to a preacher. Cracking that nut, or "original" question in life, appears to most of us to be the best chance we have at figuring out how to get rid of the trouble, pain, or evil that torments us—in much the same way that a doctor diagnoses and treats an ailment by figuring out its original source. Where did this cancer start? Why is this person having a fever? But whenever thinkers attempt to answer this big question of the origin of evil, they end up with only two possibilities: either evil itself doesn't really exist (it has no beginning at all), or God himself has no beginning, origin, or existence. It is either evil or God that we figure does not really exist. Philosophy lives on one side or the other of this extravagant either-or. First, you pick your culprit, then the source of that evil must be negated. Either evil or God must be removed from existence and cease to be. However, every attempt to think one or the other of these out of existence is not very effective therapy in the end. If evil doesn't exist, then it sure puts on a good show! If God doesn't exist, then he keeps popping up in the heads of the biggest thinkers while they are attempting to exorcise him once and for all. God doesn't die easily.

How refreshing to have an author like Pastor Landrum admit this right from the start: evil or God? Take your pick! And the "winner" gets exorcised from intellectual existence. In theology, we have a name for this kind of chutzpah. It is called "saying what a thing is," rather than what we wish it to be. That slogan comes from Martin Luther and his famous Heidelberg theses of 1518. Sometimes, this candor is called the "theology of the cross" rather than one that seeks glory. For this reason, Martin Luther is not just one among many theologians who discuss God's hiddenness (since all theologians are somehow taking up the subject). He is the consummate teacher—not because he is Protestant, German, modern, or whatever one prefers or dislikes about him but because he heard clearly what God did when he cursed, and what God does when he blesses. Luther learned God's means, or instrument, for these acts as well, which was nothing more or less than the spoken word. Moreover, Luther learned what a promise was, what God was doing by making a promise, and especially how to actually deliver this through a sinner to a sinner.

In any case, the gospel actually makes a writer bold enough to cease playing with evil as if it were a zoo animal or a virus to investigate under a microscope—from a safe distance. Anyone who is caught up in the war with evil will want to hear what this book says. It will teach you not only what a "hidden God" means or why God would bother to hide from us. Nor does it only teach the long tale of evil according to human intellect—a veritable fable of the cat chasing its tail. This book will tell you what the difference is between preached God and unpreached God. That knowledge and fact will either sink your ship or free you. Of course, I hope for the latter. In any case, the subject matter of this book is the center of all philosophy, all theology, and all psychology. It will help you understand what evil is and, for that matter, even where it comes from. More than that, it will teach you how to give and receive the salve and salvation that alone comforts a mind and a heart that have suffered evil as discomfort of conscience. The gospel, after all, is a word that defeats evil, suffering, and death. It turns out that it is the only word that can do that! Why not learn what it sounds like from reading this book? Then, you will have the hope that in your time of trial, the gospel word will be applied to you by an actual preacher. Or perhaps, even more, you will become that preacher who is used to deliver another suffering person from an unpreached God into the hands of the preached one.

The Reverend Doctor Steven D. Paulson,
Chair of Lutheran Theology,
Luther House of Study, Sioux Falls, South Dakota

Preface

Mid-December 2014 found me pushing my mother in a wheel-chair down a hallway in the senior-care facility that had recently become home for her. Lewy body dementia had robbed her of her independence, making round-the-clock care necessary. Wheeling her into her room, I fashioned a makeshift altar out of her tray table and prepared the elements of the Lord's Supper. After the words of institution, we began to pray the words our Savior gave us when—staring at the woman gazing blankly past me and mumbling incoherently—asking God to do his will on earth and in heaven stuck in my throat like cement. I literally could not speak as tears welled up in my eyes. This amazing woman who had birthed, loved, nurtured, and provided for me my entire life to this point was suffering mightily. Susan, my wife, became the preacher in that instant and confidently continued to pray until the prayer was complete. After regaining a measure of composure, I gave my mom the bread and wine as Jesus said to do, painfully aware that the only certainty I had of God's benevolence is the gospel promise given in the word and sacrament.

My experience that day confirmed yet again what I had learned from the expositions of Martin Luther's writings done by Gerhard Forde, Steven Paulson, and others. Luther was on to something with his distinction between God preached in the gospel and the terror of God not preached outside the gospel. Unfortunately, my experience also confirmed that much of the other scholarly and pastoral work about evil and suffering is, for various reasons, bogus, offering no real or lasting comfort and often making the problem worse. Against that backdrop, I offer the following work.

I've attempted to do at least two things in this book. First, I've endeavored to establish some characteristics of a Lutheran apologetic for the problem of evil and divine hiddenness before offering a preliminary sketch of the apologetic. In contrast to the bulk of thought about the problem of evil, my goal is to demonstrate the advantage of an apologetic based on Luther's thought. Second, though limited, I've attempted to actually do some apologetics. Out of necessity, I have interacted with a broad range of theologians and philosophers, thus producing some potentially complex scholarly content, but my intent for the work is pastoral. Ultimately, my prayer is for the reader to be comforted by the promise of the gospel proclaimed "for you."

The formal research and writing of my work here began with the pursuit of the MA Theology degree from Concordia University Irvine. The faculty graciously allowed me to tailor all my research papers and my final thesis around the theme of "Martin Luther's hidden God." Being able to research and write major portions of this book and have it critiqued by scholars while simultaneously earning a master's degree was immensely helpful. I want to thank the faculty and staff of Christ College, Concordia University Irvine for allowing me to study with them. Thinking together with brothers and sisters in the Lutheran Church—Missouri Synod was enlightening, challenging, and very rewarding. I am certainly better for the experience. I'm especially grateful to my faculty advisor, Dr. Daniel Deen, whose keen insight helped shape much of this work.

I would also like to acknowledge the following people. I want to thank my wife, Susan, who encouraged me to start this process and has held me accountable for finishing. It never would have gotten off the ground, much less been finished, without her support. I want to thank the dear saints of Nativity Lutheran Church, Brandon, Mississippi, for their gracious support of my continuing education endeavors. My work would have been impossible without them. A pastor couldn't ask for a finer congregation to shepherd. A hearty thank-you goes to Mr. Glen Owen, whose interest in my work prompted his considerable financial support for the project. I am grateful to Linda Skupien for courageously working through the draft and offering her editorial insights for clarity. Finally, I am grateful to the taxpayers of the United States of America for funding much of my degree through the Post 9/11 GI Bill. What a grand deal for service members who have first had the privilege of serving the citizens of this great country to then receive financial help with an education.

Scott Landrum
Reformation 2021

Introduction

THROUGHOUT HISTORY, PEOPLE HAVE wrestled with the problem of evil and posed the question in a variety of forms. Succinctly stated, why is there evil if God is all-powerful, all-knowing, and all-good?[1] The topic is complex, as the selected readings in Michael Peterson's lengthy volume *The Problem of Evil* detail; important thinkers from the disciplines of literature, philosophy, and theology struggle for answers, the certainty of which remains elusive.[2]

Modern pupils of Irenaeus tell us that evil is a tragic but necessary tool for the development of our true humanity. Augustine assures us that evil is our fault, a product of misplaced freedom. Thomas Aquinas tepidly argues that there can be no evil coming from God, while David Hume, along with his contemporary disciples, reverse the equation, beginning with evil before concluding that there can be no God. The crushed bodies of women and children piled high after the Lisbon earthquake reduce Voltaire to conclude fatalistically that "whatever is, is right." The character Ivan in *The Brothers Karamazov* cannot reconcile God's existence with the

---

1. Many argue that attempting to answer this question is ultimately futile. I am sympathetic to their concern and agree to a large extent. Lack of ultimate answers, however, does not stop the questioning. The problem of evil and divine hiddenness forces us to be theologians, but, as we will see, much of the reflection that results compounds the problem. Therefore, the nature of my work here is pastoral. I am not attempting to provide an ultimate answer to every nuance of the discussion. Instead, I am making the argument, based on Luther's thought, that proclamation of the gospel of Jesus Christ "for you" is the best way forward.

2. Peterson, *Problem of Evil*.

evil and suffering so prevalent in the world. Followers of the process philosopher Alfred North Whitehead and the like encourage us to work hard, because evil is something that can be overcome by struggle and attention to detail. We could go on with examples, but the bottom line is that at least one of two assumptions is shared by those just mentioned. Either God's existence should be denied, or his actions in the world should be explained or defended for not behaving according to law, reason, or rationale.

For theists and polytheists, who assume at least some degree of divine benevolence, the problem of evil gives no quarter. On the other hand, technically, there can be no problem of evil for atheists denying the existence of a divine being, benevolent or otherwise. Still, few, if any, escape the existential suffering produced by the presence of evil in the world. Therefore, the impact of evil is universal, affecting believer and unbeliever alike.

Divine Hiddenness

One dimension of the problem of evil is the disconcerting specter of God's hiddenness.[3] In response to the vast amount of evil and suffering in the world, one could reasonably expect God to make his presence and benevolence known by some means. Yet, no universally discernible reply is forthcoming. The resultant dilemma is called divine hiddenness. In the book *Divine Hiddenness: New Essays*, Daniel Howard-Synder and Paul K. Moser have compiled a selection of essays that treat various dimensions of divine hiddenness.[4] In his contribution to the work, entitled "The Silence of the God Who Speaks," Nicholas Wolterstorff offers an especially pertinent description of divine hiddenness, calling it "biblical silence." He describes this silence as God's refusal to answer questions of

---

3. Some theologians and philosophers treat the problem of evil and divine hiddenness separately. I recognize the difference but maintain they are two aspects of the same reality.

4. Howard-Synder and Moser, *Divine Hiddenness*.

extreme importance to those suffering, a silence made worse by the fact that God has in times past responded through Scripture.[5]

Given the gravity of the topics, one shouldn't be surprised that the problem of evil and divine hiddenness continues to be a major part of current theological and philosophy-of-religion debates. A simple search of Amazon.com yields several pages of results for books about the subject matter. Atheist and agnostic authors use the problem of evil and God's silence as proof that God, or a being like God, doesn't exist. Theists, on the other hand, offer reasonable arguments for continued belief in God despite divine hiddenness and the problem of evil. Additionally, some scholars attack the issue by constructing models of theodicy or by building a logical defense.[6] All of the scholars, both atheists and theists, analyze the problem of evil and divine hiddenness, arguing passionately and cogently, yet come to varied and sometimes opposite conclusions, signaling the difficulty of articulating a convincing understanding.

Martin Luther and the Problem of Evil and Divine Hiddenness

Martin Luther was no exception to the quandary of divine hiddenness, and reconciling God's existence and benevolence with the presence of evil in the world was perhaps his most vexing theological challenge. Far from an academic theological topic, divine hiddenness was for Luther, like all humanity, personal. Magdalena, his teenage daughter, died in his arms tragically, forcing him to wrestle with the hidden God. Luther tackled the difficulty with his teaching on the distinction between God "unpreached," or hidden, and God "preached"—that is, revealed and proclaimed in the

---

5. Wolterstorff, "God Who Speaks," 215.

6. A theodicy is a philosophical/theological argument that seeks to defend God's benevolence in spite of evil's presence in the world. A defense is a philosophical argument that, by challenging the premises of arguments for the problem of evil, attempts to demonstrate that the presence of evil and God's existence are not illogical. Those employing a defense make no claim to provide actual reasons for evil.

gospel. He explains, "We have to argue one way about God or the will of God as preached, revealed, offered, and worshipped, and in another way about God as he is not preached, not revealed, not offered, not worshiped."[7]

The interpreter of Luther commonly discovers three understandings of divine hiddenness in the Reformer's thought. One, seen most clearly in the Heidelberg Disputation, is God's hiddenness in offensive opposition to the expected. God, the dead Jew hanging wasted on a cross for the sin of the world, is the epitome of the unexpected! A second hiding place for God is the Holy Spirit's work through word and sacrament. The Holy Spirit gives faith to whom he pleases through the common means of water, bread, and wine combined with the word of the gospel spoken through the mouth of a sinful preacher. Luther writes:

> Our know-it-alls, the new spirits, claim that faith alone saves and that works and external things add nothing to it. We answer: It is true, nothing that is in us does it but faith, as we shall hear later on. But these leaders of the blind are unwilling to see that faith must have something to believe—something to which it may cling and upon which it may stand. Thus faith clings to the water and believes it to be baptism, in which there is sheer salvation and life, not through the water, as we have sufficiently stated, but through its incorporation with God's Word and ordinance and the joining of his name to it. When I believe this, what else is it but believing in God as the one who has bestowed and implanted his Word and has offered us this external thing within which we can grasp this treasure.[8]

Third, Luther refers to God as "hidden," or "not preached," denoting God acting wrathfully as penalty for transgression of the law. Oswald Bayer, whom we'll hear from later, refers to this aspect of divine hiddenness as "understandable wrath."[9] Though the

7. Luther, *Luther's Works*, 33:139.

8. Martin Luther, *The Large Catechism*, in Kolb and Wengert, *Book of Concord*, 460.

9. Bayer, *Martin Luther's Theology*, 196–97.

cause is not always recognized or acknowledged by the recipient, God's punishment for lawlessness produces suffering and death, thus hiding his benevolence.

In the following, I will focus on what I believe to be a fourth understanding of divine hiddenness in Luther's thought. Luther asserts that God acts in "naked majesty" and wills freely in deeply mysterious, often terrifying ways that transcend a reversal of expectations, use of unexpected means to proclaim forgiveness, or wrath stemming from punishment for lawlessness. God's hiddenness in this manner is unexplainable this side of the eschaton. This fourth understanding is the least understood and carries the greatest theological and philosophical implications for the aim of this work: the construction of a Lutheran apologetic for the problem of evil and divine hiddenness.[10]

In *The Bondage of the Will* and his subsequent *Lectures on Jonah, Lectures on Isaiah*, and *Lectures on Genesis*, the Reformer developed his teaching on God's mysterious and unexplainable hiding. *The Bondage of the Will* is Luther's fullest teaching on divine hiddenness, and central to Luther's theology in it is the assertion that God "foresees, purposes, and does all things according to His own immutable, eternal and infallible will."[11] Luther is writing about the comforting certainty of God's sovereignty in matters of salvation, but his teaching is fraught with philosophical and theological complexity, forcing him to wrestle with the inescapable corollary of God hiding in immutability and the terror that results. Nevertheless, he persists, because at stake is the absolute assurance

---

10. B. A. Gerrish calls Luther's understanding of hiddenness in revelation "Hiddenness I" and includes teachings such as the theology of the cross, the law, and the word and sacraments. He calls Luther's understanding of divine hiddenness behind revelation "Hiddenness II," which includes God willing and acting apart from revelation. Gerrish argues that in Luther's thought, Hiddenness I and II are distinct and antithetical (Gerrish, "To the Unknown God," 268). Organizationally, Gerrish's categories are perhaps helpful, but their usefulness is limited, because he fails to note Luther's emphasis on proclamation as the solution to the theological knot created by divine hiddenness. The reader is left at an impasse, because Gerrish doesn't provide the entirety of Luther's thought on the matter.

11. Luther, *Bondage of the Will*, 80.

that salvation is given and preserved by a promise from a radically free, omnipotent God who cannot be moved.

Luther did not like the implications of God hidden in immutability. He knew the offensiveness of asserting God necessitates all things, an offense from which even recipients of the gospel promise are not immune. Steven Paulson explains, "Immediately a person wonders about whatever might happen outside of this promise . . . If God's will is necessary, then God can be said to work evil. In that case we have a terror for God."[12] Nevertheless, Luther was convinced that God must rule all things immutably, lest the foundation of faith be removed. Although God's actions in the world are often a painful mystery, they cannot be denied. Moreover, God is immutable; they must be his will. Luther refused to speculate about this and admonished people to run away from the hidden God. That same immutability, however, applied to God revealed in the gospel, is the most comforting doctrine. Absolutely no contingency can stop God from accomplishing his will, thereby making God's promise given in the gospel unassailable. Luther insists:

> If, then, we are taught and believe that we ought to be ignorant of the necessary foreknowledge of God and the necessity of events, Christian faith is utterly destroyed, and the promises of God and the whole gospel fall to the ground completely; for the Christian's chief and only comfort in every adversity lies in knowing that God does not lie, but brings all things to pass immutably, and that His will cannot be resisted, altered or impeded.[13]

Said crassly, when it comes to God's immutable hidden rule and its importance for the giving and preserving of salvation, Luther was willing to take the bad with the good.

---

12. Paulson, *Luther's Outlaw God*, 1:169.
13. Luther, *Bondage of the Will*, 84.

The Shape of Lutheran Apologetics

Works about the problem of evil and divine hiddenness fill the burgeoning field of Christian apologetics. Unfortunately, contemporary works written from a uniquely Lutheran perspective concerning apologetics in general and the problem of evil and divine hiddenness specifically are relatively rare by comparison. Lutherans, in contrast to other faith traditions, have, for the most part, avoided formal apologetics.

A few exceptions exist, most notably the work of John Warwick Montgomery. Works such as *Christ as Centre and Circumference*, *Evidence for Faith: Deciding the God Question*, *Tractatus Logico-Theologicus*, and *History, Law, and Christianity* mark Montgomery as perhaps the foremost contemporary Lutheran apologist. In his works, he provides a vigorous endorsement of evidential apologetics and a treatment of apologetic issues using the evidential approach.[14]

Rod Rosenbladt has also established himself as an able Lutheran apologist. In his work *Christ Alone*, Rosenbladt applies his skill by demonstrating the strength of evaluating contemporary issues with the Lutheran emphasis of *solus Christus*.[15] More important than Rosenbladt's writing is his influence on a range of noted scholars and apologists. *Theologia et Apologia: Essays in Reformation Theology and Its Defense Presented to Rod Rosenbladt* demonstrates Rosenbladt's inspiration on others for the apologetic task. The essays, written by both Lutherans and scholars from other faith traditions, reveal the breadth of the apologetic undertaking.[16] The articles contained in *Making the Case for Christianity: Responding to Modern Objections* continue to demonstrate Rosenbladt's influence on the book's contributors, but more importantly,

---

14. See Montgomery, *Christ as Centre*, *Evidence for Faith*, *Tractatus Logico-Theologicus*, and *History, Law, and Christianity*.

15. Rosenbladt, *Christ Alone*.

16. Francisco et al., *Theologia et Apologia*.

the articles are written from a Lutheran perspective.[17] Overall, though, the Lutheran contribution to apologetics is scant.

Lutheran reluctance to enter the apologetic fray is understandable. Minus adherents of a presuppositional apologetic approach with their conviction that the claims of Christianity are irrefutably true and therefore beyond debate and need of reasonable argumentation, most apologetics is conducted by Christians who assume the freedom of the will to some degree. Consequently, apologetic methods often employ tactics that unwittingly appeal to a magisterial use of reason in which rationality is elevated as a primary source of authority. By utilizing archeological evidence, biblical reliability, logical and philosophical arguments, personal experience to include near-death experiences, and scientific evidence, the apologist posits the irrational character of unbelief in contrast to the reasonableness of faith. In turn, an appeal is made to weigh the evidence and make a decision to believe or not.

Classical apologetics illustrates the method perfectly. Utilizing arguments from cosmology, teleology, morality, and the like, combined with various "proofs," the attempt is made to first establish the reasonableness of God's existence before moving on to offer evidence validating the claims of Christianity. The hope is that a person confronted with the logical argumentation of this method will concede that the claims are, in fact, reasonable and choose to believe.

Lutherans, at their best, balk at such an approach, actually convinced of its opposite. The human will is not free but bound— unable and unwilling to trust God. At their core, original sinners are captivated by the belief that God, if he exists, can somehow be bought off by human effort. For the more pious, the cultivation of virtue and the avoidance of vice are thought to do the trick. For others, simply denying God's existence is all that is required. So deep is the bondage that arguments and proofs pandering to the free-will myth can do nothing to produce true faith in Jesus Christ. Apart from the Holy Spirit, who calls through the gospel, gathering, enlightening, and sanctifying God's elect, a person will

17. Maas and Francisco, *Case for Christianity.*

never confess that anathema of human reason penned by Luther: "I believe that by my own understanding or strength I cannot believe in Jesus Christ my Lord or come to him."[18]

All is not lost, however, with apologetics. Due to secularism and the religious and cultural diversity of the contemporary world, Peter's admonition to always be prepared to give a defense of the faith ought not to be dismissed (1 Pet 3:15). Who can forget *Religulous*, Bill Maher's "drive-by" attack on unsuspecting and ill-prepared Christians in which he used the debunked babblings of Gerald Massey to argue that Christianity is based in part on the Horus story of Egyptian mythology.[19] All Christians, especially Lutherans, have something to say in response to critics like Maher. Going forward, I'll argue that it is possible for Lutheran engagement in the biblical mandate to do apologetics within a prevailing culture ripe for the apologetic task while also remaining within the parameters established by the Lutheran Confessions, which deny the freedom of the will, thereby making faith solely the work of God.

Lutheran Apologetics and the Problem of Evil

Concerning the contribution of Lutheran apologists to the problem of evil and divine hiddenness specifically, Angus Menuge's essay "Gratuitous Evil and a God of Love" is significant.[20] Menuge's emphasis on "Christocentric narration" is a pioneering work in the Lutheran apologetic discussion on the problem of evil, but even his work does not incorporate Luther's teaching on the distinction between God hidden and God preached. Therefore, a uniquely Lutheran apologetic for the problem of evil utilizing Luther's teaching on God's hiddenness remains elusive. I will argue in the following pages that a robust emphasis on Luther's teaching can

18. Martin Luther, *The Small Catechism*, in Kolb and Wengert, *Book of Concord*, 355.

19. Maher, *Religulous*.

20. Angus Menuge, "Gratuitous Evil and a God of Love," in Maas and Francisco, *Case for Christianity*, 140–65.

contribute to the discussion in helpful ways. The goal of this work, then, is to begin the task of constructing a Lutheran apologetic for the problem of evil and divine hiddenness by identifying and applying key elements from Luther's thought that are essential for a Lutheran treatment of the topic.

I take as my thesis that Luther's teaching on God hidden provides the way forward in the conversation. His refusal to speculate about the will and actions of God hidden coupled with his insistence that a benevolent God is known only in the gospel of Jesus Christ proclaimed provides the parameters for discussing the problem of evil and divine hiddenness. Granted, Luther never offered a formal philosophical argument concerning evil and divine hiddenness, nor did he produce a theodicy or a formal defense. Furthermore, his contribution is thoroughly Christian and of primary use in the church catholic; nevertheless, his thought has insight that spans the breadth of the conversation—if in no other way, than to challenge much of what has been said by theologians and philosophers about evil and divine hiddenness. I contend that a Lutheran apologetic is rooted in Luther's use of Paul's argument in Rom 3:1–8. We'll see that for Luther, this passage provides limits when addressing the problem as well as the emphasis on proclamation of the gospel as the lasting solution to the universal suffering created by evil and divine hiddenness.

Beware, Luther's teaching carries implications that may not be well received. History shows us that most Lutheran theologians have minimized Luther's teaching on God's hiddenness. Though Luther considered his teaching on the matter to be of utmost importance to posterity, Lutheran theologians, by and large, have not agreed, thereby missing an essential component of his thought. We will see that Luther's teaching sometimes compliments but more often critiques post-Reformation Lutheran theologians, who, though taking his thought about the hidden God seriously, have tried to bridle its radical nature. So it goes for philosophers of religion who attempt the same. Luther's teaching almost always attacks their thought.

The angst created by Luther's teaching shouldn't be surprising. Paulson reminds us that at their best, Lutheran theology and, by extension, Lutheran apologetics perversely advocate the destruction of what is esteemed most highly by people.[21] Of highest value in this discussion is the concept of a God who behaves himself according to law and logic. Hiddenness, however, renders God uncontrollable and arbitrary, leading to the inescapable conclusion that God is in some manner related to evil. I believe this unease with God's relationship to evil is why later generations of Lutheran theologians have been reluctant to follow Luther's lead, to say nothing of Christians from other faith traditions and philosophers of religion.

John Dillenberger's survey work *God Hidden and Revealed* demonstrates that Luther's teaching has not fared well even in the Protestant theological tradition flowing from the Reformation.[22] Major branches of Protestant thought, including the Ritschlians,[23] the History of Religions School led by Rudolf Otto, the Erlangen theology, and Neoorthodoxy—whose leader, Karl Barth, infamously placed a drape over *Luther's Works*—have ignored, reinterpreted, or rejected out of hand Luther's thought.[24]

I recall vividly an uncomfortable exchange that occurred when I presented a lecture on the hiddenness of God in Luther's thought to a Christian ecumenical group. One pastor in particular—ironically, from a denomination open to just about any theological idea imaginable—became enraged at Luther's "grotesque" God, as he described it, before trailing off with "I guess I really don't know Luther!" How true. Sadly, my experience has been much the same among many Lutheran colleagues. Nevertheless, the advantage of Luther's thought and an apologetic built on it is demonstrable, as we will see.

---

21. Paulson, *Lutheran Theology*, 1.

22. Dillenberger, *God Hidden and Revealed*.

23. Albrecht Ritschl was a prominent nineteenth-century German Lutheran theologian whose central concern was the effect of the gospel on the moral actions of humanity. Followers of his thought were referred to as Ritschlians.

24. See Dillenberger, *God Hidden and Revealed*.

In the following, I will synthesize Luther's teaching on the problem of evil and divine hiddenness by first analyzing the relevant biblical material that shaped his thought and then surveying the works produced by Luther that contain his thought. Next, I'll survey some selected teachings of post-Reformation Lutheran theologians on the problem of evil and divine hiddenness and compare it with Luther's thought in order to demonstrate how Luther's thought compliments or critiques these teachings. After that, I'll survey the arguments concerning the problem of evil and divine hiddenness as well as the theodicy models of selected philosophers of religion and theologians before comparing them to Luther in order to demonstrate how Luther's thought compliments or critiques them. I'll then offer a modest, preliminary sketch of a Lutheran apologetic for the problem of evil and divine hiddenness based on the analysis and comparison. Finally, I'll apply the apologetic to a biblical test case to demonstrate the advantage of an apologetic built on Luther's thought. My work here is an opening salvo. I make no claim to be the last word on this issue!

CHAPTER 1

Martin Luther's Hidden God

Contemporary Scholarship on Luther's Thought about God Hidden

A CLUSTER OF WORKS have been produced that—if not in whole—at least in part are concerned with Luther's teaching on God's hiddenness.[1] Interestingly, the scholars who penned these works emphasize that Luther believed hiddenness is an activity of God and not simply an attribute in the manner argued by Rudolph Otto in *The Idea of the Holy*.[2] The consensus is that Luther's strong Christology produced his stress on God's hiddenness apart from the gospel. God hides so as not to be found in any place outside of Jesus Christ and the proclamation of the gospel.

A troubling aspect of God's hiddenness apart from the gospel is that God appears dualistic, but Eberhard Jüngel argues against such a notion in his work *God as the Mystery of the World: On the Foundation of the Theology of the Crucified One in the Dispute between Theism and Atheism*. Jüngel affirms that Luther believed in only one God, not two. The alien work produced by hiddenness

---

1. Lienhard, *Witness to Jesus Christ*, 255–58; Steinmetz, *Luther in Context*, 23–31; Barth, *Theology of Martin Luther*, 101–34; Paulson, "Luther on the Hidden God."

2. Otto, *Idea of the Holy*.

and the proper work produced by the gospel are both works of the same God.[3] William Placher strengthens the idea in his work *The Domestication of Transcendence: How Modern Theology about God Went Wrong*. Placher claims that hiddenness is a mere appearance with no real substance.[4]

By no means do Jüngel and Placher settle the issue. Gerhard Forde, while affirming that Luther was no dualist, argues in *Theology Is for Proclamation* that for Luther, the distinction between God hidden and proclaimed in Jesus Christ is real and not to be minimized.[5] He writes, "Thus there is a battle. It is God against God . . . The revealed God must conquer the hidden God."[6] Oswald Bayer echoes thoughts like Forde's in his work *Martin Luther's Theology: A Contemporary Interpretation*.[7] Concerning the divide between God hidden and proclaimed and the mystery it creates, Bayer writes, "The decisive point in regard to the *Deus absconditus* does not lie simply in the experience of evil but in the fact that evil is imperceptibly mixed within the good."[8] Similarly, Paulson, in his work *Lutheran Theology*, describes the hidden God as something akin to an impenetrable silence, thus agreeing with Forde and Bayer.[9]

Luther's Hidden God

"One God, two wills," Luther shockingly asserts in *The Bondage of the Will*. Luther maintains that God wills the death of the sinner and, at the same time, because of Christ, does not will the sinner's death.[10] Interestingly, *The Bondage of the Will*, along with *The Small Catechism* and a few others, were the only works Luther

3. Jüngel, *Mystery of the World*.

4. Placher, *Domestication of Transcendence*.

5. Forde, *Theology Is for Proclamation*, 22.

6. Forde, *Theology Is for Proclamation*, 22.

7. Bayer, *Martin Luther's Theology*, 196–213.

8. Bayer, *Martin Luther's Theology*, 196–213.

9. Paulson, *Lutheran Theology*, 86.

10. Luther, *Bondage of the Will*, 169–71.

thought worthy of use by posterity. In light of the importance Luther attached to his teaching contained in *The Bondage of the Will*, certain questions arise. What is the biblical basis for his teaching? What does his teaching in other works add to his assertions in *The Bondage of the Will*? Answers to these questions provide the threefold purpose of this chapter: to analyze the biblical material from which Luther derived his teaching, survey his teaching in *The Bondage of the Will*, *Lectures on Jonah*, *Lectures on Isaiah*, and *Lectures on Genesis*, and synthesize his understanding of the differentiation between God hidden and proclaimed.

A Biblical Basis for God hidden: An Analysis of Paul's Use of Ps 51:1–6 in Rom 3:1–8

As one who famously confessed to being "bound by the Scriptures,"[11] Luther's teaching on God hidden and proclaimed is anchored in the Bible, specifically Paul's theological treatise to the church in Rome. Luther writes, "This Epistle is really the chief part of the New Testament and the very purest Gospel, and is worthy not only that every Christian should know it word for word, by heart but occupy himself with it every day, as the daily bread of the soul."[12] In the epistle, Luther discovered that the righteousness of God is found in God's words. God is justified—that is, shown to be righteous—in his words. Conversely, outside of his words, God's will and actions cannot be justified by humanity.

Luther based his discovery on Paul's usage of Ps 51 in Rom 3:1–8.[13] He writes in a lecture on Ps 51, "God is not justified in Himself, but in His words and in us."[14] Luther again asserts in his Romans commentary, "God cannot be justified by any man, since He Himself is Righteousness, indeed, the Eternal Law, Judgment

---

11. "Martin Luther," para. 3.
12. Luther, *Commentary on Romans*, xiii.
13. Luther, *Luther's Works*, 10:235.
14. Luther, *Luther's Works*, 10:235.

and Truth."[15] In spite of this, Luther adheres to the passive translation of the passage from the LXX and asserts that God "stoops" by allowing himself to be justified by humanity. He explains, "But God is justified in His sayings when His Word is recognized and accepted by us as just and truthful."[16] Said another way, God's benevolence is revealed and given only through proclamation of the gospel. Furthermore, God is also judged when people do not believe his word, thereby calling him a liar, although the truthfulness of God's word is not affected by unbelief. Luther comments, "So God is justified in His sayings even by His enemies, for his Word is victorious over all."[17] Therefore, those accusing God of unrighteousness are judged appropriately.[18] This passage from Romans will be used to provide the biblical context for understanding Luther's teaching on God hidden and proclaimed.

Setting the Stage: An Analysis of Ps 51:1–6

One of the seven so-called penitential psalms, Ps 51 poetically recounts David's confession of sin and request for forgiveness prompted by Nathan's prophetic confrontation of the king. Ultimately, the psalm reveals that God's steadfast love and mercy, apart from law, is David's only hope and where his trust lies.

The psalm reads:

> For the director of music. A psalm of David. When the prophet Nathan came to him after David had committed adultery with Bathsheba.

> Have mercy on me, O God,
>   according to your unfailing love;
>   according to your great compassion
>   blot out my transgressions.
> Wash away all my iniquity

15. Luther, *Commentary on Romans*, 67.
16. Luther, *Commentary on Romans*, 67.
17. Luther, *Commentary on Romans*, 67.
18. Luther, *Commentary on Romans*, 67.

and cleanse me from my sin.

For I know my transgressions,
and my sin is always before me.
Against you, you only, have I sinned
and done what is evil in your sight;
so you are right in your verdict
and justified when you judge.
Surely I was sinful at birth,
sinful from the time my mother conceived me.
Yet you desired faithfulness even in the womb;
you taught me wisdom in that secret place. (Ps 51:1–6)

The historical context evoking the confession is David's adulterous affair with Bathsheba and subsequent murder of her husband Uriah, recorded in 2 Sam 11–12. Lurking behind David's admission of transgressing the fifth and sixth commandments—and, by extension, the entire Decalogue—is the more important confession of his sinful nature as Adam and Eve's progeny and his complete dependence on the steadfast love and mercy of God for forgiveness.

Structurally, Marvin Tate offers a helpful division of the passage under analysis:

Prayer for forgiveness	vv. 1–2
Confession of sin	vv. 3–4a
Rightness of divine judgment	v. 4b
Confession of sinfulness	vv. 5–6
Prayer for forgiveness	vv. 7–9 [outside the analysis][19]

God's righteousness, ṣĕdāqâ, occurs in verse 4b and occupies the central position of the chiastic structure found in this portion of the psalm. This suggests that God's righteousness is the key to understanding the psalm.

19. Tate, *Word Biblical Commentary*, 12

David's prayer for forgiveness in verses 1–2 begins with a probable invocation of the "mercy formula" found in Exodus: "And he passed in front of Moses, proclaiming, 'The LORD, the LORD, the compassionate and gracious God, slow to anger, abounding in love and faithfulness'" (Exod 34:6). David makes three appeals to God's character. First, he asks God for "unmerited love or favor" (*ḥānan*), particularly like that of the relation of a superior to an inferior.[20] Second, David appeals to God's "steadfast love" (*ḥesed*), best described as covenantal love, like the selfless, sacrificial love between relatives or lovers.[21] Finally, David requests "mercy" (*rāḥām*) like that of a mother for her child.[22]

Following the three appeals to God's character, three petitions for the forgiveness of David's unrighteous behavior in relationship to the covenant emerge coupled with three descriptions of his unfaithfulness. First, David asks God to blot out or obliterate (*māchāh*) his "transgression" (*pesha*), which is the offensive rejection of God's order for life. Second, David requests that God vigorously "wash" (*kābhash*) him like one washes clothes so that his "iniquity" (*'āôn*) is removed. Third, David pleads to be "cleansed" (*ṭāhēr*) like dross from metal from his "sin" (*chᵃṭā'*), or offensive deviation from the right way of life.[23]

Verse 3 begins David's confession of sin. He is intimately and continually aware that his sin is present and burdensome. David's sin doesn't come and go in his conscience; it is festering and produces fear and shame. The heart of his confession is verse 4a: "Against you, you only, have I sinned." Ultimately, all sin is against God, as David says.[24] Luther's interpretation of this verse helps. He writes, "Only and solely against Thee do I sin. In Thy sight I am nothing but a sinner. Before Thy judgment I boast of no merit or righteousness, but I acknowledge that I am a sinner, and implore

---

20. Tate, *Word Biblical Commentary*, 13.

21. Tate, *Word Biblical Commentary*, 13.

22. Tate, *Word Biblical Commentary*, 13.

23. Clifford, *Old Testament Commentaries*, 249–50.

24. Lawson, *Old Testament Commentary*, 283.

Thy mercy."[25] The exclusive confession of sin against God does not mean David thinks he has not wronged other human beings. David harmed Bathsheba and Uriah, as well as many others. The confession should be understood to mean that to sin against others is to sin against God. The parallel phrase "and done what is evil in your sight" is an all-encompassing construct signifying that David understands that his unfaithfulness transcends his adulterous and murderous immorality to include his guilt for all that is opposite of God's justice and righteousness.[26]

In light of all that David has confessed, the heart of the matter surfaces in verse 4b: "So that you are proved right when you speak and justified when you judge" (Ps 51:4b). By confronting the sinner, God is righteous, which is faithful to the covenant. David has been "repented" by God's word of law. He offers no excuse, deferring instead to God's righteousness and justice. David's lack of excuse proves that God is righteous and just in his words and actions. Thus, David is left with only a plea for forgiveness. David's bold plea with which he started his prayer, however, could only be made if God was faithful to the covenant in ways beyond the obligation of law—namely, God's steadfast love and mercy. Said another way, David's hope springs from faith in God's *ḥesed*, apart from law.

Verses 5–6 ("Surely I was sinful at birth, sinful from the time my mother conceived me. Surely you desire truth in the inner parts; you teach me wisdom in the inmost place" [Ps 51:5–6]) extend the encompassing nature of David's sin and the righteousness and the justice of God. He is confessing that there has never been a time when he hasn't "done what is evil in your sight" (Ps 51:4). Consequently, the "reliability" that God desires is impossible by David's self-effort. Furthermore, God requires wisdom, translated as the "coping ability to deal with those skills, temptations, responsibilities, and sufferings which are common to human life in ways that enhance the performance of healthy and successful living."[27]

---

25. Luther, *Luther's Works*, 12:337.

26. Tate, *Word Biblical Commentary*, 16.

27. Tate, *Word Biblical Commentary*, 17.

David knows that this, too, eludes him and thus asks God to give, or teach, what is demanded.

Establishing Paul's Parameters: An Analysis of Rom 3:1–8

Paul's letter was probably written to a mixed group of Jewish and Gentile Christians in Rome who may have been struggling with unity. Nevertheless, because the epistle is ultimately about God's righteous and merciful work on behalf of humanity, it possesses universal application and transcends the Roman context.[28]

Throughout Romans, Paul is concerned with the justification and righteousness of both God and humanity. He utilizes words built off the *dik-* stem to expresses a range of meanings for justice, justification, and righteousness in the context of a covenantal relationship. One of the heaviest concentrations of Paul's usage of the *dik-* stem is located in Rom 3, especially his employment of the thematic phrase "righteousness of God." The construct appears five times in slightly more than twenty verses, as seen in the text:

> What advantage, then, is there in being a Jew, or what value is there in circumcision? Much in every way! First of all, the Jews have been entrusted with the very words of God. What if some were unfaithful? Will their unfaithfulness nullify God's faithfulness? Not at all! Let God be true, and every human being a liar. As it is written: "So that you may be proved right when you speak and prevail when you judge." But if our unrighteousness brings out God's righteousness more clearly, what shall we say? That God is unjust in bringing his wrath on us? (I am using a human argument.) Certainly not! If that were so, how could God judge the world? Someone might argue, "If my falsehood enhances God's truthfulness and so increases his glory, why am I still condemned as a sinner?" Why not say—as some slanderously claim that we say—"Let us do evil that good may result"? Their condemnation is just! (Rom 3:1–8)

28. Middendorf, *Concordia Commentary*, 3–20.

God's righteousness is foundational to Paul's argument in this section of Romans, where, by appeals to the Old Testament, Paul strengthens his attack on sinful humanity begun in chapter 1. He specifically cites Ps 51:4b from the LXX: "That you may be justified in your words, and may overcome when you are judged."[29] This passive translation of the verse provides both the means for establishing God's righteousness—namely, his words—and his justification when judged by humanity. In light of the above, certain questions arise. What are the "words" that justify God's judging and judgment? What about God's actions outside his words—is God concerned with humanity's judgment of him there?

Structurally, Rom 3:1–8 is thought by scholars to serve a pivotal role in Paul's argument. This section looks back to Paul's prosecution of the Jews contained in 2:17–29 and also reintroduces elements found at the very beginning of Paul's attack in 1:17—namely, God's righteousness. At the same time, the passage looks forward, providing preliminary information to be explained later in the epistle.[30] Moo writes, "What begins, then as an attempt to answer an objection to Paul's ironing out of distinctions between Jews and Gentiles (vv. 1–2) becomes a frustratingly brief discussion of the relationship between Israel's unbelief and God's righteousness and, ultimately between human sin and God's purpose."[31]

Referring to his argument in chapter 2, Paul employs a series of rhetorical questions in the opening section of chapter 3. In verses 1–2, Paul asks what advantage the Jew has over the Gentile and identifies the promise of God as the answer. Before Christ, Gentiles had no promise from God. They had God's word in general revelation and were therefore without excuse, but no word of peace and grace was given to them.[32] Not so for the Jew, who was

29. Brenton, *Septuagint with Apocrypha*, s.v. "Psalm 51."

30. Middendorf, *Concordia Commentary*, 216.

31. Moo, *Epistle to the Romans*, 180.

32. The Greek philosophers illustrate the inadequacy of general revelation. Consultation of the oracle at Delphi, Plato's world of Forms, and Aristotle's prime mover are examples of philosophy's inability to discover the gospel. God's existence is evident, but his mercy and grace remain hidden. See also Paulson, *Lutheran Theology*, 1.

the object of God's sovereign election and also possessed the Old Testament scripture that included, at its heart, the promise of future salvation in the gospel.

Anticipating a fuller discussion of God's sovereign election in chapters 9 through 11, Paul asks in verse 3 if Jewish unfaithfulness will annul God's faithfulness to his promise of Israel's future salvation. Also, beginning in verse 3 and continuing through verse 7, Paul contrasts Israel's sin with God's righteousness. Israel was *epistesan* (unfaithful), displaying *apistia* (unfaithfulness), yet God displayed *pistin* (faithfulness). Paul labels Israel *pseustes* (a liar), in contrast to God, who is *alethes* (truth). Israel's *adikia* (unrighteousness) is unlike *dikaiosynen* (the righteousness of God). Finally, my lie (*emo pseusmati*) is contrasted with the *aletheia* (truthfulness) of God. Without a doubt, Paul trusts that God will remain righteous in relation to his promise in spite of Israel's failings.

The apostle's vigorously negative answer in verse 4 demonstrates his conviction that God is faithful to his promise in spite of the untruthfulness of every person, an assertion that occupies the remainder of verse 4. Paul's quotation of Ps 51 in this verse is pivotal to his continued prosecution of Jewish unfaithfulness. As we've seen, the psalm is about God's righteousness—through steadfast love and mercy apart from law, but not exclusively so. God's righteousness according to law is also included. The purpose clause in Ps 51:4b indicates that in spite of any mercy apart from the covenant, because David sinned against God, God was right to judge him according to law. Hence David's words that God is just when he judges.

Like David, Paul maintains what he previously said about God's righteousness to covenant faithfulness by steadfast love and mercy. At the same time, Paul is posturing for a continued attack utilizing God's judgment according to the law. Paul's point is that God's faithfulness to his promise should not be presumed upon by Jewish recipients simply because of ancestry. Not every Jew will be saved; nevertheless, God is faithful to the covenant, and even his judgment according to the law proves it.

Paul's rhetorical questions in Rom 3:5, 7, and 8 are meant to expose a presumably familiar objection to his theology concerning the Jews. The gist of the questions is that by electing them, God is simply using the Jews to "show off" his righteousness apart from the law.[33] Therefore, God has no right to judge Jewish unfaithfulness, since it is for his glory and they have no choice (verse 5). According to the logic of the scheme, doing evil increases God's glory and is to be preferred (verses 7–8). Apparently, this latter point is what some were accusing Paul of teaching, a claim he quickly dismisses, in light of verse 4b, with his "so what" in 5b.[34] Paul seems to be saying that even if God is using the Jews, God is still righteous, because he is God. Paulson helps to explain this, writing, "God *is* just in his inner being, and so God is always and ever God whether someone believes in him or not; lack of faith does not reduce God's righteousness even an iota."[35] It is God's righteousness in himself, in his almightiness, that is Paul's justification for explaining how God can judge all the world (verse 6) in spite of cries of injustice.

The protests are meant to push Paul's argument to absurdity, charging him with calling good/lawfulness, evil; and evil/lawlessness, good. Paul's detractors are complaining about his accusation in Rom 2:17–29. The implication is that Paul is much too pessimistic about human ability to keep the law. The Jew is wondering how he or she will ever be righteous if not by works of the law. This is a charge that goes to the heart of Paul's argument that the righteousness of God is revealed by faith in God's word (Rom 1:17), even for the Jew.

Despite the charges of his detractors, Paul persists, because he, like David, knew one's only hope of avoiding God's righteousness according to the law is to trust in God's righteousness gifted to people as steadfast love and mercy. In other words, a person's only hope is God graciously saving him or her from God. Paul makes this point explicit in Rom 3:21, explaining that the righteousness that saves is wholly apart from the law and completely a matter of

---

33. Middendorf, *Concordia Commentary*, 233.

34. Middendorf, *Concordia Commentary*, 233.

35. Paulson, *Lutheran Theology*, 55.

faith in God's word in Jesus Christ. Paul writes, "But now apart from the law the righteousness of God has been made known, to which the Law and the Prophets testify. This righteousness is given through faith in Jesus Christ to all who believe. There is no difference between Jew and Gentile, for all have sinned and fall short of the glory of God, and all are justified freely by his grace through the redemption that came by Christ Jesus" (Rom 3:21–24).

Thus, the detractor's questions are beside the point, because faith in Christ is all that matters.

Summary

The words that justify both God and people are God's words of future salvation given to the Jews in the Old Testament. In Christ, God will be judged faithful to his promise, as Paul will make abundantly clear in his argument throughout the remainder of the epistle. He uses the well-known Ps 51 to remind the Jews of David's appeal to God's steadfast love and mercy given in God's words, and those words are what provide the context of God's righteousness. He also employs the psalm to teach the universality of God's justice when he judges and when he is, in turn, judged by humanity. Paul does not give answers that justify God outside of his words of salvation. Paul's insistence that the benevolence of God is known only in God's words, coupled with his silence about God's benevolence apart from God's word of salvation, provides the parameters for discussing divine hiddenness, parameters reflected in Luther's teaching.

A Survey of Luther's Works Containing His Teaching on God Hidden and Revealed

If Luther's teaching on God's hiddenness were confined to *The Bondage of the Will*, one could argue that it is simply a polemical exaggeration created by the passionate exchange with Erasmus. Luther's teaching, however, appeared in various works over the next twenty years, spanning the length of his career and suggesting it is more than a passing thought.[36] Therefore, a survey of Luther's teaching contained in his works is in order.

The Bondage of the Will

The book is a confutation of Erasmus's argument that, due to ambiguity, a synthesis is required for the interpretation of Scripture. Christ is vacuously absent from the proposed synthesis. It is a hopeless argument comingling law and gospel. People obey God's commands and are rewarded, or they disobey and receive punishment; and assumed by Erasmus throughout is the freedom of the will. He cannot believe otherwise, lest God be unjust in giving a law to people who are unable to fulfill it. Thus, for Erasmus, obligation implies ability. He uses several Old Testament proof texts to illustrate his argument that, because of free choice, people are rewarded for obedience or punished for disobedience.[37]

Luther, in turn, focuses especially on Erasmus's misuse of Ezek 18:23: "Do I take any pleasure in the death of the wicked? Declares the Sovereign LORD. Rather, am I not pleased when they turn from their ways and live?" (Ezek 18:23). This verse, Luther argues, illustrates the humanist's inability to distinguish law and gospel. He argues that Erasmus fails to understand that God's desire for the salvation of sinners spoken of by Ezekiel is confined to God's revelation in Jesus Christ (God preached), but, apart from that revelation (God not preached), God does, in fact, will the death of sinners.[38] Pharaoh and Judas provide specific examples of God willing and working destruction in people. In this manner, Luther undermines Erasmus's argument concerning free will by asserting that because God sometimes acts unfairly, justification by a legal scheme is impossible. Sensing as early as 1518 the ambiguity of a legal scheme, Luther argued in the *Heidelberg Disputation* that

---

36. *The Bondage of the Will* was written in 1525, *Lectures on Jonah* 1525–26, *Lectures on Isaiah* 1527–30, *Lectures on Genesis* 1535–45.

37. Nestingen, "Introduction," 12–14.

38. Luther, *Bondage of the Will*, 169–71.

"the law brings the wrath of God, kills, reviles, accuses, judges, and condemns everything that is not in Christ."[39]

God's hiddenness, however, is not confined simply to his understandable wrath against those who have transgressed his law. Echoing his assertion of divine immutability made earlier in *The Bondage of the Will*, Luther writes:

> God in His own nature and majesty is to be left alone; in this regard, we have nothing to do with Him, nor does He wish us to deal with Him. We have to do with Him as clothed and displayed in his Word, by which He presents Himself to us. That is His glory and beauty, in which the Psalmist proclaims him to be clothed (cf. Ps. 21.5). I say that the righteous God does not deplore the death of His people which He Himself works in them, but He deplores the death which He finds in His people and desires to remove from them. God preached works to the end that sin and death may be taken away, and we may be saved. "He sent His word and healed them" [Ps 107:20]. But God hidden in his majesty neither deplores nor takes away death, but works life, and death, and all in all; nor has He set bounds to Himself by His Word, but has kept Himself free over all things.[40]

Troubling though it is, Luther deduces that God has two wills: one bound to the gospel of Jesus Christ proclaimed and one hidden—unbound and outside of Christ.[41] Forde writes, "A veritable battle is being fought over us between God not preached [hidden] and God preached [revealed in Christ]. God not preached devours sinners without regret, but the preached God battles to snatch us

---

39. Luther, *Luther's Works*, 31:54.

40. Luther, *Bondage of the Will*, 170.

41. Luther, *Bondage of the Will*, 170. Luther teaches double predestination in *The Bondage of the Will*. Still, his understanding should not be equated with Reformed thought, which holds that God elects some for salvation and damns others before the foundation of the world. Calvin's followers, especially at the Synod of Dort, used logic in the attempt to remove all mystery from predestination. Luther maintains the mystery by proposing that God actively damns all sinners in order to save the same sinners elected for salvation by proclamation of the gospel. Luther links election with proclamation, not eternal decrees.

away from sin and death."[42] Luther's teaching here is at the height of its offensiveness, calling to mind Wolterstorff's description of the silence of the God.[43] All that remains is suffering when God goes silent after having spoken. The writer of Ps 116 makes this even clearer, citing "affliction" as a consequence of believing what God has said.

What we are talking about here is categorical freedom ascribed to God, and such freedom is immensely troubling to finite and sinful creatures. God, in his majesty—unfettered from even his word in general, arbitrarily inflicting weal and woe—is deadly and produces what Forde labels "haunted theologies." Consequently, much of the theological enterprise is little more than an attempt to make God behave. Regardless of the offense to all, Luther continued his assertion, because he had no choice. He knew that no amount of theological, philosophical, or any other kind of doctoring—not even appeals to God's word abstractly understood—alter reality. Only the continual proclamation of the gospel to individuals in the here and now provides hope.

At the end of *The Bondage of the Will*, Luther uses an analogy of lights to illustrate God's hiddenness in contrast to his work in the gospel proclaimed. The "light of nature"[44] (human reason) can make no sense of God's actions in nature and history. The unchecked injustice and suffering present in the world reasonably call into question the goodness and existence of the God who rules all things by necessity. Is God good or evil, moral or immoral? The answers aren't clear. Luther writes, "Just see! God so governs this physical world in outward affairs that, if you regard and follow the judgment of human reason, you are compelled to say either that there is no God or God is unjust. As the poet [Ovid] said: 'Oft am I provoked to think there are no gods.'"[45]

The work of some of the greatest human minds is demonstrative of the difficulty alluded to by Luther's "light of nature."

42. Forde, *Essential Forde*, 218.

43. Wolterstorff, "God Who Speaks," 215.

44. Luther, *Bondage of the Will*, 317.

45. Luther, *Luther's Works*, 33:291.

Plato found himself on the "horns of a dilemma" here, and with the so-called "Euthyphro dilemma," he offered one of the oldest and most notable attempts at an answer. In brief, the question is whether something is right because God commands it or whether God commands something because it is right. To affirm the first premise appears to make God capricious, with the implication that morality rooted in God has no stable foundation. Affirming the second premise makes God conform to an outside standard of morality, implying that God is not omnipotent. Consequently, God is either a tyrant or simply the "middle man," neither of whom should be obeyed.[46]

Christians typically affirm that God, as the Creator of all, is not constrained by outside things or forces. Robert Adams argues that God, by his status as God, stands above morality. He does what he chooses, but his choice is not commanded.[47] Therefore, it is logical to say that God has no moral virtue in the way humans possess virtue—by obedience to commands. Consequently, Christians are less likely to affirm the second premise and so avoid that horn of the dilemma. However, such a move is not without consequence; the other horn is formidable!

As Luther noted, an arbitrary God is a problem, and repulsion to such a God is at the heart of Plato's story. An answer to Plato, modeled on Thomas Aquinas's moral theory, is the human-nature argument. The good life for humanity is thinking and doing those things that bring fulfillment. Thoughts and actions that produce good for people are a reflection of human nature as created by God. God would not be likely to command things that contradict human nature as designed. Thus, God acting arbitrarily is ruled out logically.

The problem with the human-nature argument is that God sometimes does command things that contradict the good. One of the most notorious examples is the so-called "binding of Isaac."

46. *The Westminster Dictionary of Christian Ethics*, s.v. "Divine Command Morality," 159–60.

47. Adams, "A Modified Divine Command Theory of Ethical Wrongness" in *Religion and Morality*, 339.

That event was a divine contradiction in which Abraham is tested by God. The earlier promise of the "Seed" is contradicted by God's command to sacrifice Isaac. In that event, God's word is illogically against God's word. Granted, Isaac was not killed, but God's command, which Abraham had every intention of following completely, contradicted the good and is, therefore, damaging to the human-nature argument's assertion about God's logical actions in the world. This is true even if God had no intention of Isaac being harmed. The confusion created by God is at the root of Luther's "light of nature" and illustrates the limits of human reason.

Luther and Reason[48]

In spite of human reason's limitations, throughout his works, Luther insists that reason has merit when utilized to provide organization and clarity of thought. Luther's reference to reason as the "devil's whore"[49] should not be understood to mean that he was in favor of radically separating philosophy, built on reason, and theology, based on revelation. Though faith in Christ is essential and of utmost importance, Luther was not content to retreat into the theological ghetto of fideism, supporting the use of reason and precision of argumentation instead. When commenting expressly about the apologetic task involving non-Christian religions, Luther writes, "You must use all your cleverness and effort and be as profound and subtle controversialists as possible; for then you are in another area."[50] Luther's comment reflects his call for a synthesis between faith and reason, because, as Luther said (quoted by Mark Mattes), "every truth is in agreement with every other truth."[51] Thus, for Luther, any approach that respects the proper relationship between reason and revelation should be employed.

---

48. I rely heavily on the insight of Mark Mattes in this section (Mattes, *Theology of Beauty*).

49. Luther, *Luther's Works*, 51:374.

50. Luther, *Luther's Works*, 26:29–30.

51. Mattes, *Theology of Beauty*, 34.

Luther employed the law/gospel distinction to accomplish the desired synthesis. Like law, philosophy, which is rooted in reason, aids people in determining the most advantageous thoughts and actions for the common good.[52] Philosophy, however, does not aid proclamation of the gospel in the manner of theology. Thus, Luther contends, philosophy serves theology, "not as a mistress but as a maidservant and bondwoman and most beautiful helper."[53] Theology, however, remained primary for Luther, and any philosophical attempts to "bury the risen Christ" were swiftly rejected.[54]

The primacy of theology is seen in Luther's assertion that "what is true in one field of learning is not always true in other fields of learning."[55] Using Christ's incarnation as an example, Luther demonstrates that the infinite and finite can be united yet retain the properties of both, thereby violating the philosophical axiom that the finite and infinite cannot coexist in each other. Consequently, for Luther, what is true in theology is not always true in philosophy.[56]

His assertion can lead to the conclusion that Luther is an advocate of a "double-truth" theory in which truth and falsity are discipline dependent. In response, Mattes explains that "Luther is no advocate of 'double truth' theory, but he does maintain that philosophy and theology constitute two distinct spheres with their own distinct logics."[57] More specifically, theology employs a distinct grammar created by God's action in Christ. Nowhere is this more evident than Luther's treatment of divine hiddenness, in which God can be both benevolent and unmercifully wrathful for reasons known only to God, an assertion offensive to reason and foreign to Erasmus.

Though somewhat more capable of explaining God's actions in the world, the "light of grace" (Christian worldview) is

---

52. Mattes, *Theology of Beauty*, 18.

53. Luther, *Luther's Works*, 38:257.

54. Luther, *Luther's Works*, 38:257.

55. Mattes, *Theology of Beauty*, 34.

56. Mattes, *Theology of Beauty*, 34.

57. Mattes, *Theology of Beauty*, 36.

also unable to explain God's actions completely, as his sovereign election of people for salvation eludes human reason. Free will is destroyed, and humanity is reduced to waiting on a preacher to deliver God's absolution, because, as Luther asserts, "we can do nothing."[58] When and where this happens remains God's sovereign choice and defies human logic, producing the condition Paulson calls "predestination sickness."[59] Only the "light of glory" (eschatological promise of the gospel), grasped in faith created by proclamation of the gospel, justifies God and provides the solution for divine hiddenness, not only in the future but even now.[60]

The eschatological nature of the proclaimed gospel promise is contained in both the word and sacraments. Concerning baptism, Edmund Schlink explains, "For in Baptism God encloses the entire past life of the baptized as well as that which is still in the future. The temporal sequence of events in the course of life has been eschatologically nullified in Baptism: The baptized has in Christ already experienced his future death, and the life of the one risen from the dead has already been opened for him."[61] Similarly, the Lord's Supper is Christ's last will and testament first distributed on the night of his betrayal but also "extended now through time"[62] each time it is repeated. Even preaching, when properly done, eschatologically "puts an end to the old and ushers in the new" by declaring the unconditional forgiveness of sin on account of Christ, thus "doing the text to the hearer."[63] Through proclamation of word and sacraments, trust in God is made possible and his benevolence is grasped now and forevermore. Luther writes:

> I have taught in my book, *On the Bondage of the Will*
> . . . This is how He set forth his will and counsel: "I will
> reveal My foreknowledge and predestination to you in
> an extraordinary manner, but not by this way of reason

58. Luther, *Luther's Works*, 33:191.

59. Paulson, *Luther's Outlaw God*, 167–70.

60. Luther, *Luther's Works*, 33:317.

61. Schlink, *Doctrine of Baptism*, 160.

62. Forde, *Essential Forde*, 275.

63. Forde, *Theology Is for Proclamation*, 155–58.

and carnal wisdom, as you imagine. This is how I will do so: From an unrevealed God I will become a revealed God. Nevertheless, I will remain the same God. I will be made flesh or send my Son. He shall die for your sins and shall rise again from the dead. And in this way I will fulfill your desire, in order that you may be able to know whether you are predestined or not. Behold, this is my Son; listen to him (cf. Matt 17:5). Look at Him as he lies in the manger and on the lap of His mother, as he hangs on the cross. Observe what He does and what he says. There you will surely take hold of Me."[64]

To summarize Luther's point in *The Bondage of the Will*, the Scriptures attest to God's radical and immutable sovereignty that is not controlled by a supposed human free will motivated by the expected reward for obedience to the law. Faith in Christ alone, given to those whom the sovereign God elects through the means of proclamation, produces salvation. Nevertheless, for inhabitants of the world, the specter of the hidden God who keeps himself free above all things remains.

Lectures on Jonah

Written the same year as *The Bondage of the Will*, Luther continues to clarify his understanding of the hidden God in his *Lectures on Jonah*. Through these lectures, Luther strives to explain how humans experience God hidden, arguing that through the natural order, people experience God as something not only superior to them but wrathful toward them:[65] "The captain went to him and said, 'How can you sleep? Get up and call on your god! Maybe he will take notice of us and we will not perish'" (Jonah 1:6). From this, Luther argues that in nature, people often experience God violently working against them and actively working their death and destruction.[66]

---

64. Luther, *Luther's Works*, 5:45.
65. Luther, *Luther's Works*, 19:53–54.
66. Luther, *Luther's Works*, 19:75.

I remember well the relief that flooded over me as I peered through the front door of Love Lutheran Church in New Orleans, Louisiana. I served as the pastor of the congregation, except on this particular day, I was active in my other capacity as a Navy chaplain assigned to the United States Coast Guard's Eighth District. Only days before, Hurricane Katrina had destroyed the Mississippi coast and also produced levee failures that flooded much of New Orleans. All hands were on deck to help with relief efforts. The pilots of a search-and-rescue helicopter I was riding in landed in a school playground across the street from the church. They graciously allowed me a minute to check on my place of worship. Though dark from lack of electricity, all was intact, like most of the surrounding area. Two minutes later, we crossed the Mississippi River and were orbiting the Fairgrounds area of New Orleans, searching for survivors. Nothing was intact. Floodwater extended as far as the eye could see.

The sights and smells of natural events like I've described render God hidden in creation—a reprehensible brew of confusion, just as Luther said. Trying to unmask God's will in these events, much less his benevolence, is uncertain at best, and those attempting to do so run a fool's errand.

Soon after the storm, I read an interesting newspaper article about an Alabama State congressman sharing publically his belief that the devastation wrought by Hurricane Katrina was God's judgment on New Orleans. Sounding much like one of Job's friends, with absolute confidence, he proclaimed that years of unabated immorality in the "Big Easy" had finally been punished. The man's statement was a bit odd, given the fact that the epicenter of immorality, the French Quarter, remained virtually untouched by the storm, leaving one to wonder if perhaps God's aim was off if punishing immorality was the goal. The fact is that the area of the flooding could easily have been reversed by the one who rules immutably, and why this wasn't the case, God alone knows. Believe me; immorality wasn't any less rampant on the high and dry West Bank!

In a manner reminiscent of his analogy of the "light of nature" from *The Bondage of the Will*, Luther argues in his *Lectures on Jonah* that every person experiences God through the natural order. Furthermore, reason alone is inadequate to explain God's actions in nature, especially his actions that cause suffering. Though reason may lead to belief in a higher power, it cannot produce true knowledge of God, to say nothing of faith in the gospel. About the sailors on the boat on which Jonah sought passage to Tarshish, Luther comments, "they named the true God, but there was no certainty about form or conception."[67] At best, reason without revelation creates an idolatrous attempt to appease the deity—a deity that Luther interestingly claims is ultimately the devil.[68]

A Gnostic Luther?

In connecting God's hiddenness and the devil, Luther is not flirting with Manichaeism—a necessary statement to make, because Luther has been accused of being Manichean.[69] Some even claim that Philip Melanchthon suspected that Luther suffered from a "Manichean delirium," presumably due to Luther's teaching on the hidden God, which appears to be dualistic.[70] The credibility of those asserting Melanchthon's suspicions is suspect, but his displeasure with Luther's theological and personal treatment of Erasmus in *The Bondage of the Will* is certain.[71] Nevertheless, the charges of a Manichean Luther leveled by S. J. Barnett and others appear to be nothing more than a polemic against Luther based on a misunderstanding of the Reformer's teaching on the hidden God. The critics emphasize the mystery of Luther's teaching on God hidden but fail to note that Luther's point is to make way for the centrality of Jesus Christ as the fullest revelation of God. With

---

67. Luther, *Luther's Works*, 19:11.

68. Luther, *Luther's Works*, 19:55.

69. Barnett, "Where Was Your Church," 1.

70. "Glosses Reveal," para. 3.

71. Weiss, "Erasmus at Luther's Funeral," 91–114.

his teaching, Luther is simply following the Lutheran principle of properly distinguishing law and gospel and should not be called a Manichean for several reasons.

First, Luther nowhere endorses or teaches the cosmology of Manichaeism. His Genesis commentary, as well as his teaching on the Apostle's Creed and in both *The Small Catechism* and *The Large Catechism*, are traditional renderings of the creation story and in no way reflect the understandings of Mani, the founder of Manichaeism. The Manichean system of belief was built on a cosmological myth influenced by Iranian dualism. From the Iranian system, Mani borrowed and sometimes renamed the major characters, including a primordial entity named Zervan. Called the Father of Greatness, he was the highest being and existed in the realm of light. Androgynous, Zervan bore twin principles. The primary principle was named Ohrmazd and, at the beginning of time, chose good. The second principle, named Ahriman, chose evil. Although conceived second, Ohrmazd was Zervan's chosen and therefore enjoyed a predestined advantage over Ahriman, although both principles were considered gods.[72]

Manichean cosmology is divided into three epochs, or creations. In the first, good and evil existed in two separate realms. The first realm, inhabited by Zervan, was called the World of Light. Ahriman, who inhabited the World of Darkness, noticed the realm of light and greedily attacked, resulting in a mixture of good and evil. Because of purity as the highest being, Zervan was unable to defend the realm of light and therefore called into existence the Mother of Life. She, in turn, called Primaeval Man, also known as Ohrmazd. The Mother of Life sent Ohrmazd into battle against the forces of darkness clad in armor and armed with five different shields of light. Ohrmazd was voluntarily defeated by the forces of darkness and becomes trapped in the evil, material world.

In the second creation, the Father of Greatness called the Living Spirit into existence, who, along with his five sons, moved to the edge of darkness. From there, he called to the Original Man,

---

72. The information in this section is adapted from Widengren, *Mani and Manichaeism*, 43–68.

who, in turn, called back. This "summons and response" is soteriologically significant, because it is the manner in which humanity is saved, according to Manichaeism. The Living Spirit, his five sons, and the Mother of Light extended a hand to Original Man, who grasped it and was saved from the world of darkness and returned to the Realm of Light. Although rescued, Original Man's soul remained trapped in darkness and required deliverance. Living Spirit accomplished the task by capturing the evil *archons*. He made the sky from their skin, mountains from their bones, and the earth from their excrement. The result was a universe that consisted of ten firmaments and eight orbs.

With the world created, the Living Spirit began the task of liberating the light particles. He purified the sun and the moon because they had not been tainted by darkness, turning them into vessels of light. Stars were made from the particles of light that had not been majorly tainted by darkness. Five planets were harsh, and therefore five days were harsh, with only two, Sunday and Monday, gentle. Liberation happened when a cosmic system of some sort drew out particles of light captured in nature and human souls and placed them in the moon for fifteen days. As the full moon waned, light was then transferred to the sun and eventually into paradise.

The third creation began when the Father of Light called the Third Messenger into existence. The Third Messenger sailed in the moon across the sky and displayed his nakedness to the demons. Appearing female to the male demons and male to the female demons, the Third Messenger so aroused the demons that the male demons ejaculated particles of light, resulting in the creation of plants on the earth; and the female demons prematurely gave birth to monsters that ate the plants and the particles of light they contained. Consequently, the particles of light were distributed between plants and the demonic offspring.

To recover light particles, Concupiscence was called into existence and devised a way to extract light from the *archons'* abortions. Two demons were employed. Asqulun captured all the male abortions, and Namrael captured the female. The two demons copulated and bore Adam and Eve. Thus, Adam and Eve's origins are demonic, yet they also retain light particles.

Because of the trapped light particles, the Father of Greatness was concerned with Adam and Eve's liberation and proceeded to secure it in a manner similar to that of Original Man's rescue. Adam and Eve were born blind and deaf and unaware of the light particles trapped within them. To liberate them, the Father of Greatness sent the Radiant-Jesus-Original-Man, who enlightened Adam and Eve. The descendants of Adam and Eve are all the souls that contain trapped particles of light. Mani then considered himself the great and final prophet sent by the Father of Greatness to give the necessary knowledge for people to liberate themselves from matter and become the light that is within them.

Obviously, Luther's teaching hardly reflects this Gnostic mythology of creation. Luther's teaching on the hidden God is not dualistic, especially in the Manichean sense. Unlike Mani, Luther does not teach that there are two principles of good and evil. Instead, God's sovereignty is paramount in all of Luther's teaching— some would argue to a fault!

Second, Luther does not teach that God remains aloof and untouchable in Gnostic fashion. Anthropologically, the Manichean myth asserts that humanity is trapped in created matter yet still retains the essence of light. Christologically, the myth claims that Jesus was only a prophet who taught about light and darkness, and that the Gospels are unreliable because they were falsified by Jesus's Jewish apostles, hence the need for Mani the "paraclete" and his gnosis, which is argued to have restored Christ's teaching. Soteriologically, Manichaeism asserts that salvation is found within the Manichean community by those who accept the teaching of Mani. Two classes of followers emerge, the primary being the Elect. The Elect were Mani's successors and were composed of 12 apostles, 72 bishops, and 360 presbyters. These followers practiced a strict asceticism that "sealed" them and resulted in their designation as the Elect. The Elect were to observe "purity of mouth" by abstaining from the consumption of "ensouled" things like meat and also from alcohol. "Purity of life" by renunciation of earthly property and labor was also required of the Elect lest they destroy Light that was diffused throughout nature. Finally, "purity of heart" was accomplished by refraining from all sexual activity. The second class of followers were called Hearers, who did not practice the prescribed asceticism but nevertheless hoped for salvation through reincarnation.[73]

For Luther, the opposite of the Manichean system is true. God wants to be known and justified by his creatures in his word of gospel, as demonstrated above. No credible case claiming that Luther was a Manichean can be made from his writings on creation or his contrast between good and evil. For Luther, God's wrath does indeed belong to God and not the devil. Luther does indicate that believers possess a fuller knowledge about the wrath of God that comes through the natural order. In contrast to unbelievers, at least they are able to name the creator of the wrath.

For Luther, God's wrath is not meaningless and without consequence. He is keen to remind his readers that a person who experiences God's wrath can be driven to the merciful God revealed in the gospel. Throughout the rest of the lectures, Luther explains how Jonah experienced the wrath of the hidden God but also experienced the God of mercy, an experience repeated by all people elected by God for salvation in Jesus Christ.[74] Still, the specter of the hidden God remains for all. For our purpose here, that God is known in nature as wrath is of utmost importance.

Lectures on Isaiah

"Truly you are a God who hides himself, O God and Savior of Israel" (Isa 45:15). Based on this verse, Luther's teaching about the hidden God in his *Lectures on Isaiah* develops the idea that God, apart from revelation in Christ, is incomprehensible.[75] The trials inflicted by God drive people to despair and take away hope

---

73. See Widengren, *Mani and Manichaeism*, 43–68.

74. Luther, *Luther's Works*, 19:78–80.

75. Luther, *Luther's Works*, 17:131.

in anything other than God revealed in Jesus Christ. Paulson explains, "It is not so much that God cannot be seen that concerns Luther, but that God actually and actively hides. God hides in order not to be found where humans want to find God. But God also hides in order to be found where God wills to be found."[76]

In his *Lectures on Isaiah*, Luther argues that God hides in two ways. First, God hides by doing the unexpected, like making King Cyrus a messiah. Second, God, in his alien work, actively hides in trials that he inflicts on people.[77] Luther's usage of God-sent trials is evidence of expansion in his thought about the hidden God. Previously, Luther confined the hidden God's work to the law primarily, although not exclusively, as was demonstrated in the survey of *The Bondage of the Will*. In his *Lectures on Isaiah*, however, Luther expands the vehicle of the hidden God's wrath to include trials. These trials are not the result of lawlessness but occur apart from the law and either drive sinners to despair or faith. This "alien work" of God produces different reactions in people. Some are "repented" and cling to the mercy of God. Others are driven further into sin and self-righteousness. Concerning believers specifically, God inflicting them with trials drives out self-righteousness and forces the believer to cling only to the promise of the gospel. For our work here, the key to Luther's commentary in his *Lectures on Isaiah* is the emphasis on God's hiddenness in trials in addition to God's wrathful work in the law.[78]

Lectures on Genesis

Delivered toward the end of his career, Luther continues his teaching on the hidden God with his *Lectures on Genesis*. He continues the familiar themes of God's incomprehensibleness outside of the gospel and the use of trials. Luther specifically attacks a doctrine of predestination that is divorced from election given through

76. Paulson, "Luther on the Hidden God," 363.

77. Luther, *Luther's Works*, 17:131–32.

78. Luther, *Luther's Works*, 17:131–32.

proclamation. Any decree of predestination apart from God's revelation of himself in the gospel remains trapped in God's hiddenness. About such a predestination decree, Luther reasons, "For if the statements are true . . . then the incarnation of the Son of God, His suffering and resurrection, and all that he did for the salvation of the world are done away with completely."[79] With only an abstract decree of predestination, certainty of God's election is impossible. One is turned inward in an effort to ensure election. Consequently, an existential crisis results from attempts to ferret out one's status before God using only divine decrees hidden in the secret counsel of God; hence Luther's admonition prohibiting speculation about the will of God apart from the gospel proclaimed.

In contrast to supposed decrees of predestination, Luther asserts that the promise of the gospel is to be used against God in his hiddenness.[80] Illustrative of the contention is Luther's teaching on Jacob encountering the hidden God at the Jabbok (Gen 32:24–31).

According to Luther, Jacob demonstrates that the hidden God also attacks recipients of the gospel promise. No one is immune, just as Jacob was assaulted physically and also verbally with words from the hidden God designed to create doubt in the promise of salvation.[81] Expressing the mystery of God hiding, Luther boldly equates God with the devil, noting the impossibility of differentiating the two apart from God revealed in Christ.[82] Luther counsels the believer to follow the example of Jacob and cling to the promise of the gospel even more strongly, using the word of God preached against God not preached.[83] Of note in Luther's *Lectures on Genesis* are the depth of God's hiddenness apart from Jesus Christ, the willingness of the hidden God to afflict even people of the gospel promise, and the futility and danger of seeking God in his hiddenness.

79. Luther, *Luther's Works*, 5:42.

80. Luther, *Luther's Works*, 6:43–50.

81. Luther, *Luther's Works*, 6:43–50.

82. Luther, *Luther's Works*, 7:175.

83. Luther, *Luther's Works*, 6:141.

A Synthesis of Luther's Hidden God

The following picture emerges from the survey of the pertinent works containing Luther's teaching about God hidden behind revelation. God is immutably sovereign, is not bound by law, and is actively hiding. Thus, he is not obligated to justify people based on the workings of a legal scheme. Through the natural order and trials, people—including the recipients of the gospel promise—experience God as wrath. This wrath is incomprehensible, and one cannot differentiate between God and the devil while in the midst of the suffering. Attempting to explain God in his hiddenness is both futile and dangerous. Though reason serves as an organizational principle for discussion of the hidden God, Luther gives no warrant for thinking about God beyond the parameters established by Paul's Letter to the Romans. Only in God's word proclaimed is God's benevolence established.

CHAPTER 2

Martin Luther's Hidden God and Post–Reformation Lutheran Theologians

Contending with the Lawless God

BASED ON THE RELATIVE scarcity of works by Lutheran theologians emphasizing the distinction between God hidden and God preached, it seems that the majority of Lutheran scholars ignore Luther's thought. Though the majority of theologians do not recognize his insight into divine hiddenness, the Reformer provides a significant contribution to the discussion. After a brief history of the reception of Luther's thought on the hiddenness of God, we'll see how his teaching critiques and compliments selected Lutheran theologians' scholarship on divine hiddenness.

A Brief History of the Reception of Luther's Thought about God Hidden and Revealed

The repercussions of Luther's insistence that God rules all things by immutable necessity with the consequence of divine hiddenness troubled many, including some of his closest colleagues. Paulson explains, "Fear engulfed even Melanchthon, who in later life could not stop warning his students against the 'stoical madness' of addressing 'divine necessity' and the hidden God as Luther did."[1] Following the lead of Melanchthon, the Philippists did not acknowledge Luther's teaching. Neither did the Gnesio-Lutherans, who—aside from an attempt to strengthen their position in the Synergistic Controversy with Luther's teaching on the hidden God—steadily moved away from his thought on the matter, as Robert Kolb points out in *Bound Choice, Election, and the Wittenberg Theological Method*.[2] Not surprisingly, the Formula of Concord also reflects this uneasiness with Luther's thought, as the teaching is noticeably absent in Article 11.[3]

Rejection and marginalization of Luther's teaching concerning God hidden and revealed did not end with the Philipists and Gnesio-Lutherans. The practice continued into the seventeenth century and beyond. Lutheran Scholastic theologian Johann Gerhard openly denounced the idea that God has two wills, labeling such notions blasphemous.[4] Not surprisingly, Lutheran Pietists also rejected Luther's teaching.[5]

Post-Reformation Lutheran Theologians' use of Luther's Teaching on Divine Hiddenness

In the mid-nineteenth century, Luther's teaching was rediscovered and became a topic of dialogue among some Lutheran theologians. The rediscovery sparked two different schools of thought that have continued up and into the twenty-first century. One group—represented by Theodosius Harnack, Oswald Bayer, Gerhard Forde, and Steven Paulson—argue that for Luther, God unpreached is a mysterious terror that is experienced, to be sure, but unknowable. While this school certainly acknowledges the fact of God's hiddenness as wrath experienced as a direct consequence of human lawlessness, they stress that God's hiddenness

---

1. Paulson, *Lutheran Theology*, 67.
2. Kolb, *Bound Choice*, 208–9.
3. "Formula of Concord," in Kolb and Wengert, *Book of Concord*, 640–56.
4. Gerhard, *Theological Commonplaces*, 240–41.
5. See Stein, "Philip Jakob Spener."

extends beyond God's wrath produced by transgression of the law. A second group—represented by Karl Holl, Werner Elert, and Gerhard Ebeling—confine God's hiddenness to the consequences of lawlessness. Said another way, the first group emphasizes that in addition to wrath resulting from human lawlessness, divine hiddenness is an effect of God's rule by immutable necessity, while the second group confines divine hiddenness to wrath resulting from human lawlessness, thus downplaying God's immutable rule. Said even differently, for group one, divine hiddenness is an activity of God that can be apart from law, but for the second group, divine hiddenness is only a consequence of the law's transgression by humanity. In the following, the works of these theologians will be surveyed to determine how Luther's teaching informs, critiques, and compliments their work.

Theodosius Harnack

Theodosius Harnack is credited with the revival of interest in Luther's teaching on the hidden God.[6] He is also the first Lutheran theologian we will examine who understands divine hiddenness to include God working beyond his wrath against human lawlessness. In his work *The Theology of Martin Luther*, Erlangen theologian Paul Althaus credits Harnack with "the best presentation of Luther's doctrine of the wrath of God."[7] Harnack argues that for Luther, God's hiddenness is God's wrath. He goes even further, maintaining that Luther taught that God relates to the world in two ways. Unpreached and apart from the gospel, God is radically sovereign, majestically working both good and evil in the world. The unpreached God is not unknown to the world, but his actions in the world are mystifying, leaving his graciousness cloaked in confusion and his wrath certain. In the gospel, however, God is the Christ whose promise of salvation is unassailable.[8]

---

6. Lohse, *Martin Luther's Theology*, 3.

7. Althaus, *Theology of Martin Luther*, 169.

8. Miller, *Hanging by a Promise*, 48–49.

Oswald Bayer

In the book *The Role of Justification in Contemporary Theology*, Mark Mattes describes Oswald Bayer as one of the foremost interpreters of Luther.[9] Perhaps most notable about Bayer's interpretation is his willingness to follow Luther's teaching on the hidden God. He argues, like Luther, that God outside of revelation in the gospel is an incomprehensible mystery working destruction on all creation, often apart from the law.[10] Bayer follows Luther's advice and flees from the hidden God by refusing to speculate about him, but he doesn't ignore him either. While true that God not preached will not allow himself to be known in his naked majesty, neither Luther nor Bayer can be silent about the work and will of the hidden God. The prohibition adhered to by both theologians is the attempt to comprehend, explain, and worship God outside of his revelation in Jesus Christ. Instead, they both insist that God revealed in the promise of Jesus Christ is the only place where humans can know for certain that God is gracious and merciful; therefore, he is to be sought there and nowhere else.[11]

Bayer asserts that the hidden God's destruction of creation is manifest in wrath, death, evil, and everything else that happens.[12] Reflecting on Luther's writings concerning God's relationship to evil, Bayer logically argues that God is somehow responsible for evil.[13] Luther implies as much but is more guarded, arguing that God is at work when evil takes place, but he is not at fault.[14]

According to Luther, what is known for certain about evil is that it originates in the human heart, like Jesus said (Mark 7:15). Therefore, any discussion of evil's origin apart from humanity's rebellion is speculative. What is known for certain is that God's sovereignty produces rebellion, thereby exposing and defining evil

9. Mattes, *Role of Justification*, 145.

10. Bayer, *Martin Luther's Theology*, 198.

11. Bayer, *Martin Luther's Theology*, 39.

12. Bayer, *Martin Luther's Theology*, 199–206.

13. Bayer, "God's Omnipotence," 87–89.

14. Luther, *Luther's Works*, 33:178–79.

as unbelief. Luther can say that God pushes evil forward by exposing what is already present in the human heart, even using evil to accomplish his will, yet remains free from the charge of creating evil.[15]

Regardless, little comfort is garnered by Luther's qualification, because God hidden is experienced as something hostile to and unjustifiable by humanity. This hostility is relentless and extends to Christians also. Both Luther and Bayer describe the result of God's hiddenness as the familiar but agonizing struggle of the sort Jacob experienced.[16] In sum, no person is safe from the unpreached God.

Like Luther, the law's function occupies a central place in the theology of Bayer. According to Luther, God's hiddenness is manifest in the law, which is used by God to extinguish the myth of "free will."[17] Law and hiddenness are interchangeable for Luther, though he does not collapse hiddenness into law, as demonstrated in the previous discussion of *The Bondage of the Will*. Bayer also asserts that God's hiddenness is something outside of or in addition to the law.

As law, Bayer thinks of hiddenness as God's understandable wrath. Jonah's willful disobedience and subsequent punishment provide an example in that Jonah knew why calamity came upon him and the ship. Bayer also conceives of hiddenness as a "third word" from God, alongside God's words of law and gospel. For Bayer, hiddenness, in this manner, is God's incomprehensible wrath that is not verbal and not understandable according to the law.[18] It is the dark side of God experienced as primal dread.[19]

Bayer's description of God as primal dread is reflective of Luther, who claims that ultimately, God as wrath is both the believer's and the unbeliever's experience of God.[20] Consequently, Bayer,

---

15. Steven Paulson provides a thorough and very helpful discussion of Luther's teaching on evil. See Paulson, *Luther's Outlaw God*, 1:191–243.

16. Bayer, *Martin Luther's Theology*, 39–40.

17. Luther, *Bondage of the Will*, 157, 161–63.

18. Bayer, *Theology the Lutheran Way*, 87.

19. Bayer, *Martin Luther's Theology*, 198.

20. Luther, *Luther's Works*, 19:54–55, 66–67, 75.

like Luther, rebels against the attempt to make sense of God's hiddenness and justify God's actions apart from the gospel, thereby turning theology into theodicy. Instead, he is content to say simply that God is responsible for working evil and that attempts to absolve God of it are fruitless.[21] For the believer, the problem of evil is worse. Because of the problem, God actively contradicts the believer's faith in the promise of the gospel.[22] Consequently, the believer never moves beyond total dependence on proclamation to create faith and provide hope. Like Luther, this struggle with God concerning the divide between the promise given and the contradictory experience of evil is called *Anfechtung* by Bayer.[23]

Rather than introducing something novel with his understanding of *Anfechtung*, Bayer is simply following Luther's logic at this juncture. Though Luther was guarded in asserting that God is responsible for evil, he freely admits that evil and the evil one are God's tools, and that God works all things. Thus, Bayer is demonstrating fidelity to Luther's thought here, although he is most certainly stating it more provocatively.[24] Furthermore, Luther's teaching on the three lights at the conclusion of *The Bondage of the Will* provides some impetus for Bayer to move the discussion of God's hiddenness into the realm of the problem of evil. Luther's use of the analogies "light of nature" and "light of grace" illustrate God's hiddenness and incomprehensibility. God cannot be justified by human reason (nature) or, because of *Anfechtung*, the believer's experience of grace. Only in the promise of the gospel, or "light of glory,"[25] is God justified by humanity and the certainty of his benevolence found.

Joining Harnack and Bayer are the theologians associated with Radical Lutheranism. Radical Lutheranism is the unofficial designation given to a confessional movement within the Evangelical Lutheran Church in America. The description stems from

---

21. Bayer, *Martin Luther's Theology*, 212–13.

22. Bayer, *Martin Luther's Theology*, 212–13.

23. Bayer, *Martin Luther's Theology*, 212–13.

24. Bayer, *Martin Luther's Theology*, 200–201.

25. Luther, *Luther's Works*, 33:317.

Gerhard Forde's article "Radical Lutheranism" on the occasion of the merging of the American Lutheran Church, the Lutheran Church in America, and the Association of Evangelical Lutheran Churches to form the ELCA. Forde argues that the task of the new denomination should be to proclaim the gospel radically through word and sacrament.[26]

Gerhard Forde

In *Fruit for the Soul: Luther on the Lament Psalms*, Dennis Ngien details the thought of Forde, noting Forde's expansion of Luther's teaching on the hidden God.[27] Following Luther, Forde made much of Luther's distinction between God unpreached and preached. In this sense, congruence between Forde and Bayer is noted. Forde even develops an entire systematic theology around Luther's differentiation between God hidden and revealed in his work *Theology Is for Proclamation*.[28]

Concerning God's hiddenness in opposition to the expected, Forde's book *On Being a Theologian of the Cross* is arguably one of the most successful attempts to make Luther's theology of the cross accessible to both specialists and nonspecialists alike—at least, that was my experience.[29] As a first-year PhD student at New Orleans Baptist Theological Seminary, I spent a lot of time in the library. For me, taking a break from studying consisted of walking the aisles looking at books. I stumbled on Forde's work quite by chance and picked it up because of the "cool" cover. I never put the book down, and my life changed, literally. Years of theological and spiritual struggle ensued as I was made into a theologian of the cross, a process that continues even today and will not be complete this side of the grave. In the work, Forde analyzes Luther's teaching on divine hiddenness in the law by intricately explaining how the

---

26. Forde, "Radical Lutheranism," 1–16.
27. Ngien, *Fruit for the Soul*, 71–73.
28. Forde, *Theology Is for Proclamation*.
29. Forde, *Theologian of the Cross*.

law is unable to justify sinners. Consequently, all theologies built on law keeping are theologies of glory and, therefore, under God's condemning wrath.

God's hiddenness, however, is not confined to God's wrath resulting from lawlessness, according to Forde. Rather than simply a list of commands, Forde, like Luther, expands "law" to include an experiential dimension of God's activity. Ultimately, anything that accuses and terrifies is the hidden God at work.[30] Citing Luther's commentary in his *Lectures on Genesis*, Forde writes about terror induced by "the voice" heard in the rustling of the leaves on a dark night. Additionally, the demands of family and society, tragedy, suffering, and ultimately death are cited by Forde as masks of "God the absconder," who is "a confusing, nefarious brew of presence and absence, of sheer timeless abstractions."[31] So deep is divine hiddenness that Forde offers no hope of "getting God off our backs" apart from the proclamation of the gospel.[32] Forde maintains that "outside of proclamation God is unavoidably wrathful."[33]

Steven Paulson

Forde's emphasis continues in leading contemporary Lutheran theologian Steven Paulson's work *Lutheran Theology*. He spends roughly a third of the book on divine hiddenness, stressing Luther's distinction between God preached and not preached. In *Luther's Outlaw God* volume 1, *Hiddenness, Evil, and Predestination*,[34] Paulson continues his analysis of Luther, providing a penetrating analysis of Luther's teaching on God hidden and revealed. Paulson begins with the law when writing about the hidden God and, in the manner of Luther, asserts that the law is not confined to the biblical law corpus alone but includes "voices that are 'passing

30. Forde, *Where God Meets Man*, 15–16.

31. Forde, *Theology Is for Proclamation*, 15.

32. Forde, *Theology Is for Proclamation*, 14.

33. Forde, *Theology Is for Proclamation*, 15.

34. Paulson, *Hiddenness, Evil, and Predestination*, vol. 1 of *Luther's Outlaw God*.

judgment."[35] Paulson continues, "The judge can be outside one's self like a father telling you to live up to your potential, or a written law that says, 'thou shalt not steal.' The judge can also be inside, called a conscience, holding itself to a standard of judgment."[36]

The judgment heard from the voices is none other than the hidden God of wrath, who hates sinners.[37] Paulson asserts that God actively hides, citing passages like Ps 44:24 ("Why do you hide your face? Why do you forget our affliction and oppression?") and Deut 31:17 ("I will forsake them and hide my face from them, and they will be devoured").[38] Ultimately, God's hiddenness is manifest as oppressive silence in which God says "absolutely nothing" in response to human suffering.[39]

Karl Holl

Karl Holl is the first Lutheran theologian we will survey who understands hiddenness as God's alien work confined to transgression of the law. Breaking with his fellow Ritschlians, Holl held a positive view of Luther's distinction between God hidden and revealed.[40] Other Ritschlian theologians argued that Luther's teaching on God's hiddenness is riddled with nominalism.[41] The teaching, according to them, reflects the arbitrariness of the nominalists in that God is not bound by anything, including the gospel promise. According to the Ritschlians, Luther was wrong, because his teaching violated the preeminence of God's love for humanity in Christ.[42]

---

35. Paulson, *Lutheran Theology*, 69.

36. Paulson, *Lutheran Theology*, 69.

37. Paulson, *Lutheran Theology*, 64.

38. Paulson, *Luther's Outlaw God*, 1:xiii.

39. Paulson, *Luther's Outlaw God*, 1:xiv.

40. Holl, *What Did Luther Understand*, 15–24.

41. Nominalism is a theory of knowledge that denies the reality of objective, universal principles. See Grenz, *Pocket Dictionary*, 84.

42. Dillenberger, *God Hidden and Revealed*, 12.

In response to his Ritschlian colleagues, Holl argues that Luther's teaching on hiddenness was not nominalist in the sense that God is arbitrary in his actions. Lest God be marginalized by creation, Holl asserts that Luther was right to emphasize God's sovereign will to act as he pleases, even apart from the law.[43] He cites Paul's argument concerning justification apart from works of the law as an example.[44] Holl, however, tightly links God's sovereignty with the work of Christ. He argues for a connection between God's hiddenness and wrath in Luther's thought, understanding Luther's teaching to be a distinction only between God's alien work of wrath in response to transgressions of the law and God's proper work of salvation in the gospel. In this manner, God's alien work in hiddenness is not arbitrary in the nominalist sense but rather preparatory for God's proper work in salvation. Thus, in contrast to his Ritschlian colleagues, Holl did not regard Luther's teaching on God's hiddenness and wrath as residual medieval, nominalist philosophy.

Holl differentiates between two kinds of wrath, explaining that there is "a severe and destructive wrath that is designed only to punish [and a] 'wrath of mercy' that purges and liberates."[45] He continues, "In and through wrath a love is revealed which desires the ultimate for people and which works tirelessly to this end."[46] God only humbles sinners through his hiddenness in order to justify them in Christ.[47] Thus, for Holl, there is no God willing and acting by divine necessity in all matters.

Werner Elert

Werner Elert, a member of the so-called Erlangen theologians working at the Friedrich–Alexander University Erlangen–Nürnberg,

---

43. Holl, *What Did Luther Understand*, 56–58.

44. Holl, *What Did Luther Understand*, 40–43.

45. Holl, *What Did Luther Understand*, 54.

46. Holl, *What Did Luther Understand*, 54.

47. Holl, *What Did Luther Understand*, 54.

and his colleagues were among the first twentieth-century German Protestants to take up Luther's teaching on the hidden God. Elert offers what is perhaps the most chilling description ever penned of the hidden God's deadly actions in a person's life, describing it as the time "when in the night two demonic eyes stare at him—eyes which paralyze into immobility and fill one with the certainty that these are the eyes of him who will kill you in this very hour."[48] Like Holl, Elert fails to differentiate between the two types of divine hiddenness in Luther's thought.[49] Elert acknowledges the importance of Luther's teaching on God's hiddenness as wrath before collapsing it solely into God's work through the law.[50] For Elert, God's wrath is a function of the law.[51] God is hidden in the law as judge against humanity, but this hiding in no way denotes a separate will.[52] God's hiddenness in the law is wrathful, even alien to God's work in salvation, but still, it remains an aspect of God's proper work of salvation.[53]

Gerhard Ebeling

Gerhard Ebeling, in his work *Luther: An Introduction to His Thought*, treats Luther's thought on divine hiddenness seriously and regards it as an essential component of the Reformer's theology. His thought on Luther's hidden God would seem to place him among the theologians in the first school, but this is not quite the case. He argues extensively against any true knowledge of God derived from nature and human reason, claiming, like Luther, that such knowledge is neither true nor beneficial. He even goes so far as to say that knowledge of God outside of his revelation in Jesus Christ is to know God as the devil.[54] The hidden God is inherently

---

48. Elert, *Structure of Lutheranism*, 20.

49. Elert, *Structure of Lutheranism*, 72.

50. Elert, *Structure of Lutheranism*, 72–73, 211–13.

51. Elert, *Structure of Lutheranism*, 35.

52. Elert, *Structure of Lutheranism*, 35–37.

53. Elert, *Structure of Lutheranism*, 71–73.

54. Ebeling, *Luther: An Introduction*, 234–35.

wrathful, determining all things—including good and evil—thereby rendering God incomprehensible apart from Jesus Christ.[55]

The Marburg theologian's shift occurs with his insistence that true knowledge of God is seen most clearly in the person and work of Christ, in whom God reveals himself as a God of grace and mercy. With his hermeneutic of "situation of speech," Ebeling argues that true knowledge of God is created and maintained by "word," specifically a word from God. According to Ebeling, God speaks *against* people in the word of law, *for* people in the word of gospel promise, and *with* people in a word of prayer.[56] Because true knowledge of God is created by the linguistic situation of God's word, divine hiddenness is contained in God's word of law and also in the form of opposites on the cross. In this manner, Ebeling treats the two types of divine hiddenness as one. For him, God hidden in the form of opposites on the cross is also the incomprehensible God hidden in wrath.[57] Thus, Ebeling fails to note that God hidden in divine necessity is different than God hidden in the suffering of the cross. Like Elert, he doesn't differentiate between Luther's understanding of God's hiddenness in wrath and God's hidden activity beyond the law.[58]

Luther and Lutheran Theologians on the Problem of Evil and Divine Hiddenness

Affirming God's hiddenness as an activity beyond wrath against lawlessness is more correct for five reasons. First, both Scripture and Luther recount instances of God's hiddenness apart from clear violations of the law. No reason is given for God's attempted murder of Moses (Exod 4:24); his hardening of Pharaoh's heart (Exod 7:3); his treatment of Job, whom the text calls righteous, a righteousness later affirmed by God himself in response to the

---

55. Ebeling, *Luther: An Introduction*, 240–41.

56. Ebeling, *God and Word*, 18–23.

57. Ebeling, *Luther: An Introduction*, 226–28.

58. Ebeling, *Luther: An Introduction*, 226–41.

accusations of Job's friends (Job 1:1, 42:7–9); or Judas, the fulfiller of David's Ps 41 (Acts 1:16). In his *Lectures on Isaiah* and *Lectures on Genesis*, Luther affirms that God's hiddenness in wrath and suffering is not always tied to violations of the law. This mystery is so deep as to be impenetrable, prompting Luther, when questioned about it, to say, "I do not know."[59]

Second, by strictly linking God hidden in wrath with violations of the law, theologians diminish the extent of *Anfechtung*. In Rom 10, Paul calls Christ the end of the law. The law is accomplished for Christians, because Christ fulfilled its demands. Luther comments on Paul's statement, writing, "The law says to a certain person: 'render what you owe; God has given the law that you might fulfill it, yet you have not fulfilled it, therefore you have an irate God and strict judge. Meanwhile the law does not say in what way or by whom that person can fulfill it. It cannot show him who fulfills it, until the Gospel comes and says: 'Christ has done it.'"[60] Yet, believers still experience the terrifying hiddenness of God, indicating that hiddenness is more than punishment for violations of the law.

Third, exhausting God's hiddenness in wrath against lawlessness introduces the unintended consequence of diluting the alien and proper work of God. The hiddenness of God can at least be minimized and, theoretically, eliminated by adherence to the law, thus diminishing the necessity of the cross, at least notionally. God's immutability in all matters, particularly salvation, is impinged upon.

The Lutheran Concordists exemplify the consequences of weakening the distinction between the alien and proper work of God. Their strong declaration in Article 11 absolving God of responsibility for evil clears God of causing reprobation.[61] Human lawlessness and the devil are responsible for God's hiddenness in wrath, according to them. No mention is made of God mysteriously

---

59. Luther, *Luther's Works*, 3:4.

60. Paulson, *Lutheran Theology*, 224.

61. "Formula of Concord," Epitome 11.2, in Kolb and Wengert, *Book of Concord*, 517.

working death and destruction among people through nature and incomprehensible trials in addition to the wrath generated by law-lessness. As a result, a contingency is introduced in that people, by an act of the will, are able to reject the proper work of God in the gospel. Focus shifts from God ruling by immutable necessity, and lost is the ability to affirm that everything that happens is the will of God, including salvation. The Formula of Concord is replete with "adverbial theology," indicating a shift in focus away from immutability and back to humanity in matters of salvation. Sub-jective phrases like "arrogantly despising" the gospel, "casting it to the wind," and "paying no attention" appear.[62] What these phrases mean exactly is elusive.

Perseverance in salvation is also called into question. Article 4 of the Formula of Concord states that faith and the Holy Spirit are lost through "intentional sin."[63] Luther himself, in the Smal-cald Articles, offers another example, referencing "public sin."[64] Additionally, Article 4 introduces a time element with the phrase "persistence in sin."[65] Defining the terms is again problematic. Taken together, these phrases suggest that the Concordists, in a move away from God's immutability, are teaching that salvation and perseverance in salvation contain an element contingent on human participation. This contingency is a softening of God's alien work that includes hiddenness due to divine necessity and of God's proper work revealed only in the word of the gospel.

Unbelief and apostasy lend credence to the Concordists' parting with Luther on the point of God's immutability. The Scrip-tures indicate that not every person will be saved and that apostasy is possible. Yet, God's immutability is precisely the answer to the Concordists' concern. God preached does not lie; therefore, those

62. "Formula of Concord," Epitome 11.12, in Kolb and Wenger, *Book of Concord*, 518.

63. "Formula of Concord," Epitome 4.19, in Kolb and Wengert, *Book of Concord*, 499.

64. Luther, "The Smalcald Articles," 3.43, in Kolb and Wengert, *Book of Concord*, 319.

65. "Formula of Concord," Epitome 4.19, in Kolb and Wengert, *Book of Concord*, 499.

whom God elects through proclamation are given an immutable promise. Consequently, the focus remains on what God has promised rather than speculation on possible exceptions spawned by human rebellion.

Luther and the Concordists have differing approaches to this matter. Luther, steering clear of conjecture about God apart from proclamation, emphasized God's immutable sovereignty in matters of salvation. The Concordists were concerned with absolving God of evil and acknowledging the reality of unbelief and apostasy in the abstract. One could say that Luther approached the matter pastorally, while the Concordists advanced the issue philosophically/theologically. This is not to say that Luther was unconcerned with theology and the reasonableness of the argument or that the Concordists were unconcerned with pastoral care, but rather that each had a different focus. However, given Luther's emphasis on the proclamation of the gospel as the solution to the dilemma of divine hiddenness, his emphasis on God's immutability in matters of salvation takes precedence over the concerns of the Concordists. In Luther's teaching, he directs us back to the ability of God to keep his promise against every contingency, even the unfaithfulness of a believer.

Fourth, Lutheran theologians who link God's hiddenness with violation of the law alone offer a type of theodicy model by justifying God's hiddenness to humanity: divine hiddenness is wrath against lawlessness, and God is justified in his wrath. Though partially correct, their emphasis violates Paul's parameters by neglecting the apostle's insistence that God's actions can only be justified by humanity in the gospel. Consequently, they undercut the necessity of proclamation. Bayer addresses the concern by offering of a third word of law in which God's will and actions remain a complete mystery, the inscrutability of which cannot be explained as the effect of lawlessness; it can only be suffered. Finally, instances of natural, moral, gratuitous, and horrendous evil[66]

66. Horrendous evil is a concept popularized by Marilyn McCord Adams. In brief, horrendous evil is that which causes the person experiencing it to doubt that his or her life is a great good and to be preferred to death (see

are not proportional to violations of the law, thus helping prompt some of the philosophers' arguments that will be surveyed in the next chapter.

Summary

A comparison of the Lutheran theologians in the first school, who treat God's hiddenness as wrath against lawlessness and the result of God's immutable rule, with Lutheran theologians in the second group, who confine hiddenness to wrath against lawlessness, alone reveals several things. Both groups affirm God hidden in the form of opposites in the manner of the theology of the cross. That God is hidden in his wrath against violators of the law is also a point of agreement. Yet Harnack, Forde, Bayer, and Paulson go further, highlighting Luther's teaching about God hidden beyond the biblical law corpus. God's immutability is an accusative "voice" that uses a variety of sources, including silence in the face of evil, to inflict trials and suffering on believer and unbeliever alike for reasons apart from violations of the law. Holl, Elert, and Ebeling, on the other hand, refuse to unhinge hiddenness from wrath against lawlessness. God's hiddenness in wrath is his alien work through the law, and his proper work, hidden in the suffering of the cross, exhausts God's hiddenness. They seek to contain God's hiddenness within the confines of the law's functions and thereby avoid the arbitrariness of hiddenness stemming from God's immutable rule. In spite of their efforts, given God's mysterious actions, coupled with the inadequacy of arguments attempting to confine hiddenness to wrath as a consequence of sin, God remains terrifyingly lawless, just as Luther and the theologians in the first group stress.

Adams, *Horrendous Evils*).

CHAPTER 3

Luther's Hidden God and Contemporary Philosophers of Religion

An Analysis

OFFENSE AT EVIL AND God's hiddenness in the face of it is not confined to theology. The problem of evil and divine hiddenness plagues the world of the philosophers also. Nicholas Wolterstorff poignantly exemplifies this when reflecting on the tragic death of his son in a mountain-climbing accident: "I do not know why God watched him fall. I do not know why God would watch me wounded. I cannot even guess."[1] Relevancy demands that philosophers of religion, like theologians, struggle with the issue.

Philosophers address the issue from logical, evidential, and emotional perspectives, because, as William Lane Craig points out in his work *On Guard*, the problem of evil is not a unified problem. It presents both an intellectual and emotional dilemma.[2] Their arguments are designed to demonstrate the reasonableness or unreasonableness of God's existence. Philosophers of religion and some theologians also attempt to make sense of evil and God's hiddenness by crafting theodicy models. Assuming God's existence, these philosophers and theologians construct theodicy

1. Wolterstorff, *Lament for a Son*, 67–68.
2. Craig, *On Guard*, 151–75.

models to provide meaning to the existence of both God and evil. In the following, the arguments of representatives from the logical, evidential, and emotional perspectives, along with representatives employing free-will theodicy, soul-making theodicy, and process-theodicy models, will be surveyed in order to determine how Luther's teaching critiques or compliments their work.

The Logical Problem of Evil

"Evil and Omnipotence," an article by John Leslie Mackie, offers an example of the logical version. In the article, Mackie argues that it is illogical for both God and evil to exist.[3] He reduces the logical problem of evil to a simple syllogism: "God is omnipotent, God is wholly good; and yet evil exists."[4] Mackie assumes that if the being commonly referred to as God exists, he has the power, knowledge, and desire to eliminate evil; yet, evil remains. Therefore, Mackie concludes, God does not exist. He qualifies his argument by saying that certain modifications in the definitions of "power," "good," and "benevolence" solve the logical problem of evil. Nevertheless, utilizing a strict definition of terms logically leads to God's nonexistence.[5]

In response, atheist Paul Draper argues that though God must operate by logic to be reasonable, it is at least epistemically possible that an omniscient, omnipotent God could allow evil and suffering for reasons known only to him by virtue of his status as God.[6] Thus, it does not follow that God, though omniscient and omnipotent, would eliminate evil. Nor does evil impinge on God's benevolence, because of the possibility of some good acquired only through suffering evil. Draper's critique seems to be that Mackie argues as if he knows the mind and will of God fully, an impossibility given human finiteness.

---

3. Mackie, "Evil and Omnipotence."

4. Mackie, "Evil and Omnipotence," 82.

5. Mackie, "Evil and Omnipotence," 82.

6. Draper, "Arguments from Evil."

Attempting logically to reconcile God's omnipotence and omniscience with the reality of evil, Alvin Plantinga joins Draper's critique by offering "free will" as the morally sufficient reason for God allowing evil. In *God, Freedom, and Evil*, Plantinga offers perhaps the most well known example of a defense, asserting that evil could be the result of humanity's misuse of free will. Though possible for God to create a world devoid of evil, morally responsible people must be free to make moral choices. Therefore, the presence of evil does not disprove the existence of God as normally defined. Granted, Plantinga is not arguing that free will is the reason for evil. He does not claim to solve the problem of evil but rather offers an argument demonstrating that the presence of both God and evil is not illogical.[7] The strength of his argument is that free will at least demonstrates a logical possibility for both God and evil to exist.[8]

The Evidential Argument from Evil

William Rowe provides an example of the evidential version of the problem of evil. In his book *Philosophy of Religion: An Introduction*, he argues correctly that the world is filled with dreadful, unwarranted evil, the rationale of which remains a mystery to humanity. Rowe asserts that, given the pervasiveness of natural and moral evil in the world, belief in God is unreasonable. He grants that perhaps God may have justifiable reasons for some evil, but given the sheer enormity of evil in the world, it is reasonable to think that humans would know what God's reasons are, but humans do not, which leads Rowe to conclude God does not exist.[9]

Rowe fashions an argument asserting that an omnipotent, omniscient, and benevolent God could prevent such evils and, because of his ability as God, not lose a possible rationale for evil, such as a greater good or free will of the sort Plantinga offered.

---

7. Plantinga, *God, Freedom, and Evil*.

8. Plantinga, *God, Freedom, and Evil*, 30.

9. Rowe, *Philosophy of Religion*, 113–15.

Furthermore, a benevolent God not only could but would have prevented evil and still been able to preserve some greater good; but because evil exists, God is unable, unwilling, or both. Thus, God, benevolent or otherwise, does not exist.

In their essay "Evil Does Not Make Atheism More Reasonable than Theism," Daniel Howard-Snyder and Michael Bergmann counter with an argument akin to that of Draper. God, by definition, always remains beyond human capacity to understand. Therefore, humans are not epistemologically capable of judging God, including his allowance and use of evil. Although God's justifying reasons for permitting evil appear hidden, humanity's failure to grasp these reasons does not mean that justification does not exist. Therefore, evil does not make belief in God unreasonable.[10] John Feinberg goes further, arguing for "uses of suffering" available to God for the possible production of a greater good.[11]

The Emotional Problem of Evil

Far from simply a logical or evidential problem confined to the domain of intellectuals, evil is also an existential problem. The Reverend Charles Jacob's "terrible sermon" in Stephen King's popular novel *Revival*[12] and the adventures of the Reverend Jesse Custer in his search for the "God who is missing" in the trendy graphic novel *Preacher*[13] are two examples of evil's ability to afflict humanity, even in the world of entertainment. Worse, life in the "real world" is marked by the trauma of both moral and natural evil that is universal in scope.

Known also as the moral problem or pastoral problem, the emotional problem of evil and divine hiddenness is perhaps the most familiar and also most difficult to define. Because suffering is universal, the demand for answers and relief is an integral

10. Howard-Snyder and Bergmann, "Evil Does Not Make."

11. Feinberg, *Many Faces of Evil*, 477–87.

12. King, *Revival*.

13. Ennis, *Preacher*.

component of humanity, and God's silence in the face of suffering is ripe for human judgment of God, in the manner of Job. Not surprisingly, atheists and agnostics alike have gained much traction in their works by focusing on the emotional dimension of evil. New Testament scholar Bart Ehrman is an example. *God's Problem* is a withering attack on what he perceives as the Bible's inability to explain the emotional dimension of the problem of evil—suffering. Ehrman argues that in the Bible, God's authoritative revelation of himself, God ought to provide answers for the suffering experienced by humanity; yet, only mystery remains, prompting Ehrman to conclude that God, if he exists, is irrelevant.[14] In spite of his skill at questioning the legitimacy of the Bible and thereby constructing a case against belief in God, Ehrman's unbelief originates in his emotional inability to reconcile God's existence with the presence of evil and suffering.[15]

Other agnostics and atheists capitalize on the emotional problem of evil and use God's hiddenness as proof that God, or at least any being worthy of the title, doesn't exist. Even more vitriolic than Erhman, in style at least, is the work of the so-called "New Atheists."[16] These men attack religion in general and Christianity in particular for a variety of reasons, including lack of scientific, rational evidence for God's existence and the historical and contemporary crimes perpetrated by religious people in the name of God. Although often unacknowledged by them, offense at God's hiddenness figures prominently in New Atheists' writing, as Paul Copan demonstrates in his work *Is God a Moral Monster?*[17]

Richard Dawkins, a popular spokesman for the group, writes, "The God of the Old Testament is arguably the most unpleasant character in all fiction: jealous and proud of it; a petty, unjust, unforgiving control-freak; a vindictive, bloodthirsty ethnic cleanser; a misogynistic, homophobic, racist, infanticidal, genocidal, filicidal,

14. Ehrman, *God's Problem*.

15. Ehrman, *God's Problem*, 1–19.

16. Richard Dawkins, Daniel Dennett, Sam Harris, and the late Christopher Hitchens are the popular face of neo-atheism.

17. Copan, *Moral Monster*, 15–23.

pestilential, megalomaniacal, sadomasochistic, capriciously malevolent bully."[18] With his emotional rant about God's supposed immorality in general and specifically in the Old Testament, Dawkins demonstrates Luther's point about God's hiddenness. People are bound to recoil from the God who creates the problem of evil and divine hiddenness.

Darwin, Dawkins, and the Hidden God

In an effort to deal with divine hiddenness, Dawkins places his trust in Charles Darwin, who also struggled with the reach of an illogical God. Darwin's *On the Origin of Species*[19] is arguably the most sustained and popular attempt to mitigate the terror evoked by God's sovereignty. Darwin sought solace in theoretical explanations of "mother nature," as if perceived knowledge about natural processes coupled with renaming the problem of sovereignty provides protection from a God who keeps himself free over all things. In other words, Darwin appears to believe that answers to the "how" questions translate into answers for the troubling "why" questions. Dawkins concurs, as we will see in the following.

Dawkins also illustrates the necessity of proclamation. In the context of a discussion about Pascal's wager, he writes, "I can decide to go to church and I can decide to recite the Nicene Creed, and I can decide to swear on a stack of bibles [sic] that I believe every word inside them. But none of that can make me actually believe if I don't."[20] Dawkins correctly demonstrates that belief isn't a matter of the will. In sum, what troubles him is God's sovereignty. In response, Dawkins follows Darwin by turning to creation, offering that nature's complex beauty creates a sense of "transcendent wonder" for humanity.[21] To explain nature's origins, Dawkins constructs a six-premised argument that is woefully inadequate

---

18. Dawkins, *God Delusion*, 242–43, 247–48.

19. Darwin, *Origin of Species*.

20. Dawkins, *God Delusion*, 130.

21. Dawkins, *God Delusion*, 33.

both philosophically and theologically. In the following, we'll see that the argument fails to remove both divine hiddenness and the necessity of proclamation.

First, Dawkins asserts that "the greatest challenge to the human intellect . . . has been to explain how the complex, improbable appearance of design in the universe arises."[22] Second, he argues that attributing the appearance of design to a designer is natural.[23] When considering human-made articles, people are logically justified to link a designed entity to its designer. Third, Dawkins maintains that the logic of premise two fails when applied to the complex design of the universe, because the "designer hypothesis" introduces more complexity into the discussion, forcing one to wrestle with the quandary of "who designed the designer."[24] Fourth, according to Dawkins, Darwinian evolution by natural selection provides the greatest explanatory power for the complexity observed in nature. Dawkins claims that Darwin and his successors have demonstrated that complexity is an illusion and the result of a slow, evolutionary process from simplicity to complexity.[25] Fifth, Dawkins grants that no equivalent to the explanatory power of evolution by natural selection has been discovered in the field of physics. Sixth, Dawkins argues that given the cosmological anthropic principle, which holds that the laws of physics governing the universe must be friendly for life, hope exists that eventually, an explanatory equivalent for use by cosmologists will be discovered. He argues that regardless of the current weakness of the argument created by the absence of no explanatory equivalent, when stabilized by the anthropic principle, the argument is stronger than the God hypothesis.[26] Therefore, Dawkins concludes, "God almost certainly does not exist."[27]

---

22. Dawkins, *God Delusion*, 188.

23. Dawkins, *God Delusion*, 188.

24. Dawkins, *God Delusion*, 188.

25. Dawkins, *God Delusion*, 188.

26. Dawkins, *God Delusion*, 188.

27. Dawkins, *God Delusion*, 189.

Working from the "failed" God hypothesis, Dawkins launches an analysis of the widespread religious phenomena observed among humans. He blames entities of cultural transmission labeled *memes* for the existence of religion. These "brain viruses" create beliefs like the possibility of surviving one's death, God being the supreme virtue, faith being a virtue, and beauty reflecting the divine, as well as creating the ability to believe "weird things" like the Trinity that aren't capable of being understood.[28]

Dawkins goes on to argue that religion is useless for human progress. He counters the idea that religion's greatest perceived contribution is morality, arguing that in reality, Darwinian evolutionary theory provides reasons for morality, including genetic kinship with its care of those with similar genetic makeup, reciprocation, and displaying generosity to acquire a good reputation, thereby displaying superiority.[29] When these reasons are combined with studies that show there is no difference between the moral decision-making of atheists and religious believers, religious people selectively derive their morals from their holy books, and religious teachings are often masochistic, then religion's futility is self-evident.[30]

Concluding his analysis, Dawkins argues that religion is harmful to human progress. He claims religious fundamentalism's demand for unquestioning faith teaches humanity to ignore the scientific method of observation and change. Terrorism is often the result of such religious "brainwashing." Therefore, he concludes, although there are gaps in human knowledge, religion is not the best explanation for the unknown.[31] Though the arguments of other neo-atheists may be more measured in tone, they agree with Dawkins that God's hiddenness certainly justifies agnosticism, if not atheism.[32]

---

28. Dawkins, *God Delusion*, 230–34.

29. Dawkins, *God Delusion*, 251.

30. Dawkins, *God Delusion*, 308.

31. Dawkins, *God Delusion*, 405.

32. See Dennett, *Breaking the Spell*; Harris, *Letter*; Hitchens, *God Is Not Great*.

Five areas of critique are offered in the following. First, Dawkins's argument seems to be logically flawed. His abductive inference that God almost certainly does not exist cannot be supported by his six premises. Granted, Dawkins has made the argument that one should not simply infer God's existence based on the appearance of design in the universe, but that does not prove God's improbability. Other arguments offered by theists that have nothing to do with design demonstrate the logical possibility of God's existence. In spite of Dawkins's critique of both,[33] Anselm's ontological argument and C. S. Lewis's moral argument provide two examples.

For many, God's existence is not based on arguments at all. Religious experience and divine revelation provide two examples. For Lutherans in particular, arguments for God's existence are viewed as suspect and always secondary to the proclamation of the gospel through the means of word and sacrament. At best, apologetic arguments lend evidential support for proclamation but are certainly not essential. Dawkins seems to have concluded that arguments from design are the sole authority for determining God's probability, and that is not true.

A second example of Dawkins's error in logic begins in his third premise and continues into the fourth. In premise three, he asks, "Who designed the designer?" His question is problematic, because it violates the philosophical principle of inference to the best explanation. Absolute certainty of some things is unattainable by humanity, resulting in the necessity of choosing the best explanation available based on explanatory power, explanatory scope, plausibility, and less ad hoc. The best explanation does not need an explanation to be valid. Requiring an "explanation of the explanation" results in an infinite regress in which nothing could ever be explained. Applying Dawkins's logic to his assumption in premise four, the evolutionary process ultimately needs an explanation from cosmological origins. Dawkins admits that such an explanation does not exist, thus begging the question of whether evolutionary theory is the best explanation for complexity.

33. Dawkins, *God Delusion*, 103–9, 241–67.

Furthermore, evolutionary theory is not without problems. The evolutionary principle of common ancestry is complicated by the fossil record, indicating that human complexity appeared early in the evolutionary process rather than later, as expected. The human capacity for language and speech and the absence of "missing links" provide other examples that evolution is still a theory and may not be the best explanation, thereby countering Dawkins's argument.[34]

Dawkins's third premise is further weakened when considering divine simplicity. He assumes that a designer is as equally complex as that which is designed. Thus, explanations of the designer would be similarly complex, leading to the infinite explanatory regress mentioned previously. God, however, when defined as creator/spirit, is simpler than his creation. God is certainly capable of great creative complexity but remains simple ontologically. Perhaps, God's self-identification to Moses in the burning bush makes the point best. Dawkins's premise seems to reveal a very narrow understanding of God, at odds with philosophical and theological thought.

Second, Dawkins's treatment of the God hypothesis appears inconsistent. Dawkins criticizes Alister McGrath's argument against him concerning scientific overreach.[35] McGrath works within the "non-overlapping magisteria (NOMA)" framework coined by Stephen Jay Gould. Stated succinctly, the NOMA principle holds that science and religion are concerned with different subject matter, and practitioners of each should remain within the confines of his or her expertise.[36] Dawkins argues, against McGrath, that science can empirically study God. Furthermore, science has found no empirical evidence for God's existence, leading to the conclusion that God does not exist. Dawkins, however, is reluctant to assert anything other than that God "almost certainly does not exist."[37] One wonders why Dawkins remains tentative

34. House and Holden, *Charts of Apologetics*, Chart 61.

35. Dawkins, *God Delusion*, 78–79.

36. McGrath, *Dawkins' God*, 80–82.

37. Dawkins, *God Delusion*, 189.

here when he is quite certain about the empirical veracity of the scientific method regarding evolutionary theory in other places.

Third, Dawkins is an intelligent scientist, so it appears he is simply unwilling to recognize the limits of science. Dawkins is correct that nature's complex beauty does create a sense of "transcendent wonder" for humanity.[38] The problem with nature is the God who creates hides behind creation, thereby forcing humanity to create idolatrous worldviews. As we saw above, hiddenness is not an attribute of God but rather an activity, as he hides from attempts to find him outside of his revelation in Jesus Christ. One shouldn't be surprised that scientists have concluded that God's existence can neither be proven nor disproven utilizing the tools of science. When considered from a faith perspective, science affirms what God has said about himself outside of his revelation in Jesus Christ.

Alan Chalmers has convincingly argued that scientific methodology does not occur in a vacuum.[39] Scientists begin with certain biases and theories that preclude total objectivity. Nevertheless, when properly practiced, the scientific method minimizes the skewing influences of the scientist. When scientists stick with "just the facts" and submit their findings to objective peer review, factual knowledge of the matter observed is highly probable, but such knowledge is never guaranteed, as Dawkins seems to believe.

Interestingly, the objective nature of scientific inquiry has aided the reasonableness of a first cause for the universe, which is central to premises five and six of Dawkins's argument but unimportant to him. Rigorous analysis has led most contemporary science to confirm the plausibility of the theory that the universe had a beginning.[40] Consequently, reliance on the "eternal universe theory," along with a plethora of other theories—some of which Dawkins commends—that assert the cosmos had no beginning, has given way to the affirming the soundness of the Standard

38. Dawkins, *God Delusion*, 33.
39. Chalmers, *This Thing Called Science.*
40. McGrath, *Mere Apologetics*, 96–98.

Model.[41] Scientists' affirmation of the universe's beginning logically points to a first cause, but such a cause remains outside the capability of scientific observation. Perhaps these findings explain Dawkins's and others' tentativeness to claim with certainty that the cause doesn't exist. Therefore, rather than prove God's nonexistence, science must leave open the possibility of the divine and the reasonableness of belief in it, yet Dawkins fails to acknowledge this reality.

In *The God Delusion*, Dawkins seems to be practicing scientism. Scientism is the optimistic belief that, given enough time and resources, science can answer all of humanity's important questions, or at least those questions deemed important by those operating in the realm of scientism. As such, scientism ceases to be pure science and becomes a hybrid endeavor that derives presumed certainty in one sphere (metaphysics) based on relative certainty in another (findings of science).[42] The late Christopher Hitchens illustrates this, writing, "Religion has run out of justifications. Thanks to the telescope and the microscope, it no longer offers an explanation of anything important."[43] The assertion's fallacy is that it exceeds the scope of scientific inquiry by offering metaphysical speculation based on material observation. The practice is dangerous, because while it appears to be science, it is little more than the biases and agendas of the one engaged in it.

A materialist, atheistic/agnostic worldview is often based on the shaky foundation of scientism. Examples abound of the inconsistencies produced by the sketchy foundation produced by scientism, with none more glaring than avowed evolutionists arguing for compassionate morality. "Survival of the fittest" by definition excludes compassion. Often, appeals to utilitarianism are made as the corrective to nature's brutality or, in Dawkins's case, his assertion of "Darwinian misfiring."[44] These appeals do little to ease the contradiction, because the natural world is littered with numerous

---

41. Craig, *Reasonable Faith*, 140.

42. Hinson and Caner, *Popular Encyclopedia*, s.v. "Science and Faith," 437.

43. Hitchens, *God Is Not Great*, 282.

44. Dawkins, *God Delusion*, 253.

illustrations of organisms, including humans, not behaving in a utilitarian fashion but rather according to the "selfish gene." These examples are far more numerous than any Darwinian "hiccups" in the evolutionary process, and they indicate a pattern rather than an anomaly. One only need observe a hummingbird feeder or a food line for starving people to see this. The rational explanation for the inconsistency is that biases and agendas have been mixed into the assertions. Critics of Dawkins and Hitchens argue that these men's arguments are weakened by the use of scientism.[45]

A fourth critique is Dawkins's careless treatment of religion. He commits the logical fallacy of hasty generalization by arguing that religious fanatics and terrorists represent all religious believers. His examples of abortion-clinic bombers and "rapture" Christians, as he calls them, are certainly not representative of Christianity as a whole.[46] Furthermore, his failure to distinguish major differences between world religions is unacceptable in any serious discussion. Religious diversity is obvious, and the beliefs and practices of different religions are enormous. Dawkins's move is troubling, given his careful defense of Hitler's dubious faith being representative of Christianity while downplaying Stalin's overt nonbelief representing atheism.[47] One wonders what happened to Dawkins's demand for scientific rigor and objectivity.

Fifth, Dawkins is critical of blind faith and the explanatory power of a "God of the gaps," arguing that things like science, art, human friendship, or humanism might provide a more appropriate substitute.[48] Dawkins is correct in saying that blind faith is problematic. His assertion applies to Christianity and all other religions. Granted, the central event of Christianity, the resurrection, is a matter of faith; nevertheless, belief in the resurrection is not fideism.

Jesus of Nazareth's crucifixion is very seldom questioned by contemporary historians. Even skeptic John Dominic Crossan

45. Eagleton, *Reason, Faith, and Revolution*, 6.
46. Dawkins, *God Delusion*, 341–46.
47. Dawkins, *God Delusion*, 308–16.
48. Dawkins, *God Delusion*, 388–420.

argues that the crucifixion is "as sure as anything historical can be."[49] Furthermore, most concur that Jesus was buried, although agreement ends there. What happened next is the subject of considerable debate. Those Christians supporting a historical resurrection argue that Jesus's followers discovered the empty tomb a very short time after his burial. Furthermore, many of those followers experienced a personal encounter with the risen Christ, which led them to conclude that Christ had been resurrected. Perhaps the most important of those encountering the risen Christ was the Christian antagonist Saul of Tarsus, whose unexpected Christian apocalypse and subsequent missionary activity make a compelling case for the resurrection.

Of course, skeptics dismiss Christian claims, arguing that the followers of Jesus were biased in favor of the resurrection and therefore compelled to varying degrees and for various reasons to perpetuate a myth.[50] To counter the Christian claim, a host of theories have been proposed and fall into two major camps.[51] The first to be surveyed here can be labeled "occupied-tomb theories." Those arguing for the occupied-tomb theory claim that Jesus could have been buried in an unknown tomb, making it impossible for Jesus's followers to know where he was buried. A variation of the theory is that Jesus's followers mistook a vacant, empty tomb for the burial place and simply surmised that Jesus must have been resurrected. Still, other skeptics argue that the historicity of the resurrection is irrelevant, because the event was invented to build legitimacy for the early church. Also denying the historicity of the resurrection are those who claim that Jesus was raised spiritually while his body remained in the tomb or that the resurrection appearances were simply the hallucinations of Jesus's distraught followers.

Each of these objections can be answered logically. Even if Jesus's followers didn't know or were mistaken about the tomb's

---

49. Crossan, *Jesus: A Revolutionary Biography*, 145.

50. Dawkins, *God Delusion*, 122.

51. This survey of major skeptical theories concerning the resurrection and reasonable responses was compiled from House and Holden, *Charts of Apologetics*, Chart 55.

location, the Roman and Jewish leaders most certainly knew. In the interest of peace, they would have been compelled to show that Jesus was still dead to counter the resurrection claims. Demonstrating that Jesus's tomb was still occupied would also have mercifully helped delusional Christians who thought they saw the resurrected Christ either bodily or spiritually. Moreover, proof of the occupied tomb would have squashed the legitimacy of the early church's claims. In summary, simply producing the dead Jesus would have destroyed the reasonableness of Christian claims. The fact that nobody did when the situation so warranted is evidence that they could not, thus demonstrating that occupied-tomb theories do not make belief in the resurrection unreasonable.

The second group of theories can be labeled the "unoccupied-tomb theories." Skeptics in this group often argue that Jesus and his disciples conspired by use of a fake death and resurrection to "trick" people into the belief that Jesus was the Messiah. Jesus was accidentally killed in the plot, forcing one of his disciples to act as the risen Christ. A second conspiracy theory is that Jesus's disciples simply stole the body and perpetrated a fraud. A third type of theory is called the resuscitation or swoon theory. Jesus, according to the theory, did not die on the cross and was able to recover with the aid of burial spices and the coolness of the tomb.

Knowledge of the historical situation surrounding Jesus's life provides damaging evidence to the unoccupied-tomb theories. The Roman army was famous for its discipline and ruthless ability to accomplish the mission. Therefore, the suggestion that Jesus did not die on the cross is incredible. Furthermore, given the proficiency of Roman ability to administer death by crucifixion, the only way Jesus could have survived was if the soldiers allowed it. One struggles to understand how and why they would do such a thing. Similarly, the suggestion of a Roman detachment's dereliction of duty by consenting to another being crucified in Jesus's stead, sleeping on post, or allowing the disciples to open the tomb and steal the body undetected is far-fetched.

The Jewish understandings of messiah also call into question the reasonableness of the theories. A crucified messiah counters all known Jewish expectations.[52] Furthermore, a lack of civil unrest because of Jesus's crucifixion implies that many Jews were hostile or, at least, ambivalent to his movement and unconvinced that he was a messiah. Consequently, the disciples' claim that the empty tomb demonstrates that Jesus was the resurrected Messiah alone would not have been convincing to their fellow Jews. Nor would the appearance of a physically battered messiah pretending to have died and been resurrected make much of an impression. Therefore, unoccupied-tomb theories are unconvincing and do not make belief in the historical resurrection unreasonable.

A third line of argument demonstrating the reasonableness of belief in the resurrection is the behavior of the disciples following the crucifixion and burial. One struggles to understand what would motivate Jesus's followers to perpetrate a resurrection hoax. No monetary advantage was gained. Their social status did not increase. Paul's power and status in Pharisaical Judaism decreased significantly. Vocationally, their lives most likely became more complicated and physically hazardous. Moreover, their boldness in spreading the resurrection story led to persecution and probable martyrdom. Why a person would be willing to die for a hoax of their creation that provided no personal advantage is deeply mysterious. Something happened to these people, and Jesus's resurrection is a very reasonable explanation.[53]

The biblical witness is a fourth plank in an argument demonstrating the reasonableness of belief in Jesus's historical resurrection. The historical trustworthiness of the biblical record is at least, if not more, sound than other ancient documents, a fact that is demonstrable but here assumed.[54] The Bible provides content that affirms Jesus's historical resurrection. According to the biblical record, Jesus was crucified and died and was buried. This reality caused his disciples great despair, fear, and confusion. A few days later, the tomb was discovered empty, and Jesus's followers experienced literal appearances of the resurrected Christ. The

52. Smith, *Old Testament Theology*, 410–16.

53. Craig, *Reasonable Faith*, 342.

54. Craig, *Reasonable Faith*, 334–37.

disciples were transformed from disillusioned followers into bold witnesses, and the historical resurrection was at the center of their preaching. Moreover, the disciples began to preach in Jerusalem, where Jesus had been buried. Logically, if their claims were not true, opponents would have simply produced the corpse. Instead, the church grew; Sunday, resurrection day, became the primary day of worship; and even skeptics like James and persecutor Saul believed.[55]

This summation demonstrates that the event is central to the biblical witness. Therefore, given the event's importance in this historically reliable document, the reasonableness of belief in the resurrection based on the Bible and the other arguments surveyed above is established. The survey I've just presented above does not provide absolute proof for the resurrection, but it does demonstrate that belief in the resurrection is not irrational, which is the charge leveled by many skeptics against Christians.

Given the nature of Dawkins's scholarship, the findings of history should be important to him. Furthermore, primitive manipulation of nature, ancient cave drawings, and evidence of communities demonstrate that humanity has, in some form or fashion, from very early on, enjoyed substitutes for the divine, like Dawkins proposes.[56] Still, the need for the divine, along with religion, persists among humans, suggesting that people aren't flawed for at least acknowledging some higher power. Dawkins seems to argue against himself with his assertion that science now and in the future will provide all the necessary answers to human questions. Given the questionable objectivity of science mentioned above, Dawkins's choice for a substitute seems to be a matter of taste, resulting in faith in a "science of the gaps."

In *The Hiddenness Argument: Philosophy's New Challenge to Belief in God*, J. L. Schellenberg offers an emotional argument that is more reasonable and philosophically precise than the arguments of the popular-level New Atheists, such as Dawkins.[57] He cen-

---

55. House and Holden, *Charts of Apologetics*, Chart 58.

56. Dawkins, *God Delusion*, 388–420.

57. Schellenberg, *Hiddenness Argument*.

ters the problem of divine hiddenness squarely in the emotional dimension, defining divine hiddenness as "the absence of some kind of positive experiential result in the search for God."[58] He argues that sincere people seek God only to find silence and suffering instead. In every other human relationship, unreciprocated love and affection leads to the conclusion that no relationship exists. Schellenberg maintains that God, by definition, must be loving and relational; yet, God does nothing to establish a positive relationship in the face of evil, in spite of some people sincerely searching. Therefore, he concludes that God, as defined, cannot exist.

Hiddenness, like Schellenberg describes, prompts the atheist philosopher Slavoj Žižek to call God the "ultimate harasser."[59] Žižek recognizes that God's hiddenness is offensive because it forces humanity to live with a God that cannot be confirmed and reverenced nor denied and put away. Even God has a problem with God, according to Žižek. Following the lead of G. K. Chesterton in *Orthodoxy*, Žižek writes concerning Jesus's cry of dereliction from the cross: "For a brief moment, God himself does not believe in himself."[60]

Of course, atheists and agnostics' conclusions based on logical, evidential, and emotional arguments are not the end of the matter. Theists, while acknowledging the problem of divine hiddenness, also offer reasonable, cogent arguments affirming God's existence in spite of divine hiddenness. One such argument, "Divine Hiddenness Does Not Justify Atheism," written by Paul K. Moser in response to Schellenberg, asserts that divine hiddenness is not a sufficient reason for atheism. Contra Rowe, who argues in his book that one cannot appeal to an expanded form of theism that includes claims from some specific religion, Moser persists, unapologetically identifying God as the Hebraic God of the Bible.

58. Schellenberg, "Divine Hiddenness Justifies Atheism," 30–41.

59. Žižek and Gunjević, *God in Pain*, 34.

60. Žižek and Gunjević, *God in Pain*, 188. Concerning Jesus's cry, Chesterton writes even more boldly, claiming that God seemed to be an atheist briefly (Chesterton, *Orthodoxy*, 145).

From there, he asserts that the proper knowledge of God is contained in revelation that is both practical and ethical. Rather than locate God's relationship with humanity in universal displays of power that remove divine hiddenness and the problem of evil, Moser relocates God's relationship with humanity in the character transformation of some individuals. He argues that God's existence and his relational benevolence are demonstrated in people who manifest a biblical ethic. Consequently, God remains hidden when searched for in universal displays of power, but he is revealed clearly in the character transformation of believers. Thus, transforming love is evidence of God's existence.[61]

Michael Rea, professor of philosophy at the University of Notre Dame, offers a nuanced approach to the existential problem of evil. In his book *The Hiddenness of God*, Rea narrows the problem of evil, limiting the conversation to talk about divine hiddenness exclusively.[62] He describes divine hiddenness as "a problem of violated expectations. We expect certain things of God in light of what we know about God and in light of a wide range of background assumptions about the world . . . But God does not deliver on our expectations; so, we are conflicted."[63]

The solution, Rea maintains, is two tiered.[64] First, any discussion of God must include talk of God's transcendence. God and his attributes elude human understanding and are known analogically.[65] Therefore, certainty about God's attributes, particularly divine benevolence, remains elusive. Consequently, humans are in no position to judge God and are better served by adopting a position of humility by curbing expectations about God's *non-revealed concepts*.[66]

Rea continues the humility theme, arguing that God is not primarily oriented to human beings but rather pursues his own

61. Moser, "Does Not Justify Atheism."

62. Rea, *Hiddenness of God*.

63. Rea, *Hiddenness of God*, 25.

64. Rea, *Hiddenness of God*, 8–9.

65. Rea, *Hiddenness of God*, 51.

66. Rea, *Hiddenness of God*, 57–62.

interests, which include humans. Thus, God's actions, while perfect and justified, are not necessarily ideal from a human perspective.[67] In the first tier of his argument, Rea seems to be simply echoing God's word spoken through the prophet Isaiah: "For my thoughts are not your thoughts, neither are your ways my ways," declares the Lord (Isa 55:8).

To this point, Rea's argument fails to address the lack of any "positive experiential" relationship with God posited by Schellenberg, to say nothing of the fury streaming from the New Atheists. The argument actually makes matters worse. Far better existentially if God doesn't exist than for him to remain hidden and absent, with "I'm God and you're not—deal with it" as the only explanation. Of course, Rea is aware of this problem and attempts to address it in the second portion of his argument.

He does so by asserting that God is not as hidden as it appears. In fact, experiencing God is a learnable skill grasped most clearly in natural and psychological phenomena. Sensory override like that experienced by Christian mystics, natural stimuli attributed by the recipient to be of supernatural origin, and sensations of the divine presence are cited by Rea as examples of God's immanence. Awareness of this immanence, then, is a matter of spiritual seeking and discipline.[68] With the addition of protest and lament, Rea contends that even those who have endured an abusive religious experience or suffered religious trauma can also find God if they are willing to seek him.[69]

Luther and Philosophers of Religion on the Problem of Evil and Divine Hiddenness

Key differences concerning the relationship of reason and revelation, the parameters for addressing the problem of evil and divine hiddenness, and the necessity of proclamation to reveal

---

67. Rea, *Hiddenness of God*, 87–9.

68. Rea, *Hiddenness of God*, 135.

69. Rea, *Hiddenness of God*, 161–79.

the benevolence of God are present between Luther and philosophers of religion employing logical, evidential, and existential arguments. Unlike those philosophers, Luther assumes a general revelation of God's existence and considers it a self-evident truth apart from human reason. He writes, "That there is a God, by whom all things were made, that you know from his works."[70] Additionally, the offense that divine hiddenness presents to human reason does not render God nonexistent. Said crassly, God is God whether one believes it or not, and the reality of suffering reveals his disregard of human reason's judgment of him. The advantage of Luther's thought is an avoidance of the wishful thinking present in the philosophers' arguments.

Furthermore, the philosophers' magisterial use of reason renders their arguments beside the point of most importance. Luther identifies the heart of the issue when he explains, "God himself, who he is, what sort of divine being he is, and how he is disposed toward you—this you can never discover nor experience from the outside."[71] Mark Mattes states the matter succinctly, writing, "For Luther, the existence of God is never in doubt. But God's disposition toward humankind is."[72]

The uncertainty of God's disposition towards humanity is why Luther begins discussion with a warning against speculation on divine hiddenness. Remaining within the parameters established by Paul, Luther admonishes people to seek God in the gospel. What is known of God for certain is what God reveals exclusively through the suffering of the cross proclaimed.[73] Only in the word of the gospel are God's actions able to be justified by people.[74] Referring specifically to Paul's argument in Rom 3:4, Luther writes:

> There is a difference between the two statements: "God is justified" and "God is justified in his sayings or works," for God cannot be justified by any man, since He Himself

70. Becker, *Foolishness of God*, 40. Luther is translated here by Becker.
71. Becker, *Foolishness of God*, 40.
72. Mattes, *Martin Luther's Theology*, 33.
73. Luther, *Luther's Works*, 31:40–41.
74. Luther, *Luther's Works*, 7:175–76.

> is Righteousness, indeed the Eternal Law, Judgment,
> Truth. But God is justified in his sayings when His Word
> is recognized and accepted by us as just and truthful.
> This takes place when we believe in His Word (*Gospel*).[75]

Yet, the philosophers constructing the logical, evidential, and existential arguments surveyed above speculate about divine hiddenness without the gospel, and their arguments end with the hidden God, whose actions cannot be justified and whose existence cannot be believed. Instead of beginning with revelation, the philosophers begin "from below." Their arguments originate from the experience of evil as they reason upward to the divine. The pro-theistic counterarguments share the same weakness. They, too, begin with divine hiddenness, and though the reasonableness of God's existence and benevolence is maintained, God's actions remain hidden. Human finiteness, free will, and lack of spiritual discipline and practice are reasons deduced for the reality of divine hiddenness, yet nothing definitive is offered, and answers remain speculative at best, because the arguments are divorced from proclamation.

Unbridled human reason informed by the senses is the method employed by the philosophers surveyed above to attain knowledge of God apart from proclamation of the gospel. Luther was critical of reason employed in this fashion and also of the philosophies that result.[76] For him, philosophies built on reason and theologies built on revelation remain divided. Mattes writes, "Undoubtedly, Luther puts his finger on an irresolvable tension between philosophy and theology, especially as the latter is obliged to articulate faithfully the gospel as *promissio* (of which philosophy knows nothing)."[77] This absolute separation prevents peering into the "invisible things of God"[78] from the ladder of the arguments surveyed above.

75. Luther, *Commentary on Romans*, 67.

76. Luther, *Luther's Works*, 31:42.

77. Mattes, *Martin Luther's Theology*, 15.

78. Forde, *Theologian of the Cross*, 71. The "invisible things of God" is a Lutheran phrase used commonly.

Luther's dependence on the parameters established by Paul remains unreasonable for the atheistic philosophers of religion. Rather than remaining silent about God apart from his word, J. L. Mackie claims that the presence of both evil and divine hiddenness and an omnipotent, benevolent God is "positively irrational."[79] William Rowe argues that given the amount of horrendous evil in the world, even God's existence is probabilistically impossible, to say nothing of his benevolence.[80] Similarly, Schellenberg asserts that divine hiddenness makes belief in a benevolent God logically impossible.[81]

Luther must also appear odd to those on the other side of the issue. Moser looks inward to some moral transformation to mitigate God's hiddenness, while Rea places the matter squarely in the hands of any earnest seeker willing to try hard enough to peer behind the veil, thus calling to mind Paulson's description of spiritual "Peeping Toms" who seek to find God in his naked majesty rather than clothed in his words.[82] Neither escapes the attempt to keep sinful humans as the active subject while forcing God to be a passive object. In other words, the arguments of both Moser and Rea remain captive to a legal scheme in which God and people are justified apart from the gospel alone. Increasing morality and positive spiritual experiences, while noble, are not substitutes for proclamation of the gospel. God absconds from all such attempts, leaving those seeking God in the manner of Moser and Rea with nothing but questions spawned from the round-trip journey in one's head characteristic of naval-gazing theology, cursed to wonder just how successful attempts to rip the mask off the hidden God have been. Those seeking God in this fashion cannot be certain they have encountered God or the devil.

An incident Luther once reported to have experienced illustrates the folly of mystically seeking God outside of the parameters established by Paul. Luther recounts:

79. Mackie, "Evil and Omnipotence," 81.

80. Rowe, "Evil Is Evidence," 11.

81. Schellenberg, "Divine Hiddenness," 41.

82. Paulson, *Luther for Armchair Theologians*, 108–12.

Christ once appeared visible here on earth, and showed his glory, and according to the divine purpose of God finished the work and deliverance of mankind. I do not desire that he should come once more in the same manner, neither would I he should send an angel unto me. Nay, though an angel should come and appear before mine eyes from heaven, yet it would not add to my belief; for I have of my Savior Christ Jesus bond and seal; I have his Word, Spirit, and sacrament; thereon I depend, and desire no new revelations. And the more steadfastly to confirm me in this resolution, to hold solely by God's Word, and not give credit to any visions or revelations, I shall relate the following circumstances:—On Good Friday last, I being in my chamber in fervent prayer, contemplating with myself, how Christ my Savior on the cross suffered and died for our sins, there suddenly appeared upon the wall a bright vision of our savior Christ, with the five wounds, steadfastly looking upon me, as if it had been Christ himself corporally. At first sight, I thought it has been some celestial revelation, but
· I reflected that it must needs be an illusion and jiggling of the devil, for Christ appeared to us in his Word, and in a meaner and more humble form; therefore I spake to the vision thus: Avoid thee, confounded devil: I know no other Christ than he who was crucified, and who in his Word is pictured and presented unto me. Whereupon the image vanished, clearly showing of whom it came.[83]

Perhaps Bayer illustrates the difference between Luther and the philosophers best, writing, "People by nature have their own natural idea of God, in which they flatten everything out to make it fit the concept of the One, the True, the Beautiful, and the Good. But the theologian of the cross has had that false idea of God shattered through painful disillusionment."[84]

---

83. Luther, *Compend of Luther's Theology*, 57.
84. Bayer, *Theology the Lutheran Way*, 190.

Models of Theodicy

Some philosophers and theologians are not content to confine the problem of evil to arguments for and against God's existence. While acknowledging the troubling aspects of evil, these scholars assume God's existence and benevolence. Their ambitious task, therefore, is constructing a model that removes divine hiddenness by helping make sense of the reality of both God and evil. About their work, Mark S. M. Scott writes, "The technical term *theodicy* signifies the defense of divine justice in the face of evil. It employs logical strategies to 'justify the ways of God to men,' that is, to vindicate God from moral culpability. More broadly, theodicy denotes the attempt to explain or make sense of suffering."[85]

Polymath Gottfried Leibniz coined the term, and those using this method to defend God offer reasons for him causing or at least not preventing evil. Historically, scholars have offered numerous models of theodicy. In addition to Mark Scott's work, a survey of the books *Encountering Evil: Live Options in Theodicy* by Stephen Davis and *God and the Problem of Evil: Five Views* edited by Chad Meister and James Dew Jr. narrows theodicy models to three primary types and two variants.[86] Free-will, soul-making, and process models are the major offerings, and each will be surveyed below.

Free-Will Theodicy

The fall narrative in Gen 1–3, combined with Augustine's commentary on this passage, serves as the foundation of free-will theodicy. Adherents begin with the assertion that God's creation was good initially. In order for creation to be good, it must be moral, because a moral universe is superior to one that is immoral or amoral. Consequently, persons were endowed with free will in order to make moral choices. Beginning with some angels, the misuse of free will spread to humanity until all became imperfect by rejecting God's goodness. This misuse of free will introduced

85. Scott, *Pathways in Theodicy*, 56.
86. Davis, *Encountering Evil*; Meister and Dew, *Problem of Evil*.

moral and natural evil into creation. Evil, however, is not an entity but rather a lack of the good. Evil has no ontological existence but is instead a manifestation of humanity's improper use of the good resulting from an abuse of free will. In the end, God, through Christ, will judge creation by saving the obedient and damning the rebellious. Adherents of the free-will model attempt to shift moral responsibility for evil to people and away from God. Evil does not hide God but is merely the consequence of misusing free will.[87]

Seeking to affirm both free will and the sovereignty of God, a nuanced version of free-will theodicy is labeled the Molinist view. Based on Luis Molina's theology of providence, adherents of the Molinist view assert that God, in his natural knowledge and middle knowledge, knows all actions that are possible for free creatures as well as what free creature will actually do in any given set of circumstances. Consequently, God's creation, including the evil within it, is the best possible world because people are genuinely free, and even though God does not will evil, its presence means he must have a morally justifiable reason for permitting it. Consolation is found in trust that God must know what he's doing even though his motives are not obvious.

Soul-Making Theodicy

Loosely reflecting the thought of Irenaeus and Origen, John Hick, in his book *Evil and the Love of God*, constructs what can be called soul-making theodicy. The premise of Hick's argument is that suffering is essential for development of the human species. God created the world good but not complete or perfect, leaving room for human spiritual and moral development. Through evolutionary means, God guided human development until the capacity to exercise free will, coupled with the capability of mature relationships characterized by love and benevolence, was possible.

Hick argues that evil's origin is the struggle of all life to develop. It is a combination of the manner in which God created

87. Augustine, *City of God*, 244–68; Plantinga, *God, Freedom, and Evil*, 10.

and sinful human choices. Evil is necessary, because it provides a demanding environment that produces suffering. Humans would not be driven to reach their full potential as the image of God without suffering. Therefore, evil does not hide God but is a necessary component of humanity reaching its full potential.

Using an analogy from child-rearing, Hick writes, "[Human children] grow to adulthood in an environment whose primary and overriding purpose is not immediate pleasure but the realization of the most valuable potentialities of human personality."[88] Hick then couples the necessity of evil and suffering with universalism. God will continue to labor with people both presently and eschatologically until all persons eventually choose the good and are thereby brought into a right relationship with God.[89]

Process Theodicy

Process theodicy, based largely on the insights of process philosophy, denies the omnipotence of God. God is not a transcendent Creator who fashioned the world ex nihilo. God, instead, is panentheistic. He is neither omnipotent nor omniscient in the traditional sense. Instead, he shares his power with other created entities, and his knowledge reciprocally increases as he and other entities have new experiences. The universe in which experiences occur is evolving, continually changing, and in a process of development created by the free choices of entities, including God and finite people. God, therefore, is unable to prevent evil, which in process theodicy has no redemptive value and is always negative. Hope exists that good choices will outnumber evil choices until evil is overcome by synthesization in God's consciousness. Process theodicy, in contrast to soul-making theodicy, asserts that there is genuine evil operative in creation that is not necessary for creation's development but that instead hinders it. Evil impedes the "maximal harmonious intensity," which is God's desire for

88. Hick, *God of Love*, 258.
89. Hick, *Death and Eternal Life*, 243–47.

enjoyment.[90] Consequently, God and humanity are required to cooperate to overcome evil in creation in order to enjoy a greater existence marked by freedom, love, and creativity.

Open-theist theodicy is a variation of process thought. Built on Clark Pinnock's work *Most Moved Mover: A Theology of God's Openness*, open-theist theodicy differs from process theodicy in only one discernible way—namely, God's sovereignty. God, in process thought, is not sovereign; therefore, he has no control over evil. In contrast, those espousing an open-theist theodicy argue that the presence of evil is simply the consequence of God's sovereign openness to allow humans true freedom.[91]

Luther and Scholars Employing Theodicy Models

Luther is at odds with theologians and philosophers who use theodicy to reconcile divine hiddenness with God's benevolence. Minimizing Paul's parameters in Romans, a free-will theodicy approach is problematic, because it offers no real insight into the problem of evil and divine hiddenness. Since humans are "good," as Genesis states, then only a deficiency in creation could account for their trespass. Appealing to the misuse of free will does not solve this dilemma, because ultimately, the problem rebounds on God for choosing to create a world where the possibility of evil exists. This regress illustrates that adherents of the model have not moved beyond divine hiddenness.

Furthermore, freedom as the morally sufficient reason for God permitting evil is suspect. In *The Bondage of the Will* and *Lectures on Genesis*, Luther argued that free will was not God's intent for humanity, and the tree of life and the tree of the knowledge of good and evil were not designed to offer a choice. Instead, the tree of the knowledge of good and evil was designed by God to be a place of worship for Adam. It was a place where, by leaving the tree alone, Adam could give thanks for God's blessings received in

---

90. Cobb and Griffin, *Process Theology*, 70.
91. Pinnock, *Most Moved Mover*.

the tree of life, thereby reverencing properly the God who stood apart and over him.[92] Thus, hearkening back to Paul's parameters, Luther's thought offers no attempt to reconcile evil's ambiguity and God.

The soul-making theodicy model is problematic also. Hick attempts to demonstrate God's benevolence with an "ends justify the means" approach. By claiming that evil is instrumental and suffering necessary with solace in universal salvation, Hick thinks to have unmasked a benevolent God. Similarly, process-theodicy models deny the necessity of the gospel. God, as "fellow sufferer," offers very little hope and ultimately returns humanity to law in order to eradicate evil. Both models minimize the necessity of the gospel's proclamation, in contrast to Luther, who locates God's benevolence in God's word alone.

Summary

Philosophically, for Luther, divine hiddenness remains impenetrable by human reason. Speculation about the hidden God, divorced from God's revelation of himself in the gospel, renders God's existence and actions in the world unjustifiable by human reason. Furthermore, theodicy models that attempt to reconcile divine hiddenness by providing reasons for the hidden God's actions ultimately fail, because they remain speculative and severed from proclamation. For philosophers of religion who speculate about divine hiddenness and those who attempt to explain it apart from the gospel, Luther's hidden God remains unreasonable and meaningless.

92. Luther, *Luther's Works*, 1:94–95; *Bondage of the Will*, 150.

Conclusion

Toward a Lutheran Apologetic for the Problem of Evil and Divine Hiddenness

WE'RE IN A POSITION now to offer a preliminary sketch of a Lutheran apologetic for the problem of evil and divine hiddenness. So far, we've seen how Luther, utilizing Paul's argument in Romans, reconciled God's immutability and God's benevolence by differentiating between God preached in his word of gospel and God not preached, hiding outside the gospel promise. We've also seen how Luther's thought has not fared well with most Protestant theologians and even some post-Reformation Lutheran theologians who insist hiddenness is confined to God's alien work in the law. We've seen how the philosophers of religion surveyed reject Luther's teaching about the God who remains illogical and irrational in hiddenness. We've also seen that theodicy models offer no real answers to the problem, and that constructing speculative rationales actually increases the dilemma of reconciling God's sovereign immutability and his compassion. In the following, I'll offer two functions of a Lutheran apologetic before providing a sketch of a Lutheran apologetic for the problem of evil and divine hiddenness, followed by a biblical test case.

Functions of a Lutheran Apologetic

Throughout this work, we've seen that a result of the impenetrable mystery of God's hiddenness is the necessity of the gospel to reveal the benevolence of God. Paulson explains, "All creatures have a relation to God not preached [hidden], but only those who have a preached God [revealed] experience his mercy."[1] The analysis of Paul's argument in Rom 3:1–8 and Luther's use of it demonstrated that faith in Jesus Christ alone is how God is judged by humanity to be gracious and merciful. Luther goes further, writing, "This is clear: He who does not know Christ does not know God . . . God can be found only in suffering and the cross."[2] Consequently, two functions of a Lutheran apologetic for the problem of evil and divine hiddenness emerge. The first and primary function of a Lutheran apologetic for the problem of evil and divine hiddenness is to aid proclamation. A negative corollary is to limit the certainty of what can be said about the hidden God.

Apologetics is for Proclamation

A Lutheran apologetic serves ultimately to aid proclamation of the gospel. Toward the end of his career, a shift is discernible in Luther's language about God. In his commentary on Genesis, he refers to God in his hiddenness as the "uncovered" or "unveiled" God.[3] Luther's words prompt Gerrish to write, "His language clearly indicates that, at this point, the image of God fades into sheer negativity: the *deus nudus* is God in himself, a strange, terrifying, unapproachable abstraction."[4] Luther's language reflects his admonition of refraining from speculation about the hidden God in the manner of the theologians and philosophers above, as well as the proper way of speaking for God. God must be preached for his benevolence to be known. Luther writes:

1. Paulson, *Lutheran Theology*, 24; italics removed.
2. Luther, *Luther's Works*, 31:53.
3. Luther, *Luther's Works*, 2:47, 276.
4. Gerrish, "Unknown God," 267.

Would to God that we could gradually train our hearts to believe that the preacher's words are God's Word and that the man addressing us is a scholar and a king. As a matter of fact, it is not an angel or a hundred thousand angels but the Divine Majesty Himself that is preaching there. To be sure, I do not hear this with my ears or see it with my eyes; all I hear is the voice of the preacher, or of my brother or father, and I behold only a man before me. But I view the picture correctly if I add that the voice and words of father or pastor are not his own words and doctrine but those of our Lord and God.[5]

Again, Luther states: "The mouth of Paul, the apostles, and the preachers is called the mouth of God . . . . The Word is the mouth of God."[6] Through preaching, then, the word that justifies God and humanity is given. Hence Luther's instruction: "Nothing except Christ is preached."[7]

Luther's understanding is captured in Article 5 of the Augsburg Confession, which states, "To obtain such faith God instituted the office of preaching, giving the gospel and the sacraments. Through these, as through means, he gives the Holy Spirit who produces faith, where and when he wills, in those who hear the gospel."[8] A Lutheran apologetic aids the pastoral task of proclamation by exposing the fallacy of all attempts to explain divine hiddenness apart from proclamation, thereby putting the gospel forward as the only "unmasking" of the hidden God.[9] In contrast, law-keeping arguments based on a magisterial use of reason and theodicy models do the opposite. Harm is done by the thought that the hidden God can be pacified with lawfulness, made reasonable or nonexistent with arguments, or defended by a rationale for his behavior.

---

5. Luther, *Luther's Works*, 22:526.

6. Luther, *Luther's Works*, 17:257–58.

7. Mueser, *Luther the Preacher*, 16.

8. Kolb and Wengert, *Book of Concord*, 40.

9. Montgomery, "Defending the Hope," 10.

By parading as a surrogate for proclamation, theodicy is especially dangerous. God is "let off the hook" by the Augustinian model by appeals to free will. The necessity of proclamation is undermined, because the hidden God is not as terrifying and the gospel not as necessary when only humans are to blame for evil. Similarly, with appeals to humanity's role in eliminating evil coupled with universal salvation or God as a "fellow sufferer," both soul-making theodicy and process theodicy impinge on God's sovereignty and make proclamation superfluous. Consequently, a Lutheran apologetic concludes by giving way to the faith-creating proclamation of the gospel as the only certainty of God's benevolence.

The Limiting and Limited Functions of a Lutheran Apologetic

Because a Lutheran apologetic ultimately exists to aid proclamation, it is limiting, because it challenges those who claim to solve the problem of evil and divine hiddenness apart from proclamation of the gospel. As we've seen, the consequence of God's immutable rule is a mystery, and those attempting to deny God's hiddenness outside the gospel or to "explain" his relationship to evil fail. "This gouty foot laughs at your doctoring" is how Luther put it when writing in response to Erasmus's attempt to "cure" the problem of divine hiddenness created by God's necessitating will.[10] In Luther's time, like today, gout was an excruciatingly painful condition. Unlike today, a doctor poking and prodding the feet of the afflicted was common, rendering the treatment worse than the disease. No relief resulted from the doctors' effort; hence Luther's saying. So it goes for all attempts that say too much about God in his hiddenness.

Collapsing the problem of evil and divine hiddenness solely into punishment for lawlessness, declaring God's existence unreasonable in the face of evil and hiddenness, or ferreting out some

10. Luther, *Luther's Works*, 33:53.

perceived meaning from it are all examples of speaking when silence is required. In spite of these attempts, the hidden God remains untamed, and the suffering created by his hiding continues unabated. This suffering, in its various dimensions, is common to all and produces a desire for hope. Thus, the universality of "suffering divine things" is a beginning point of contact for the apologetic task, but only the beginning, and it never progresses beyond functioning as law.[11] While in the midst of suffering, certain hope is not provided by apologetics.

Given the reality of suffering and the folly of attempting to explain the hidden God, a Lutheran apologetic should attack all attempts to "unmask" the hidden God. Luther argues in his *Lectures on Isaiah* that the trials inflicted on people by the hidden God are intended to drive people to despair and away from hope in anything other than God revealed in Jesus Christ.[12] He makes the same point in his *Lectures on Genesis* by citing the promise of the gospel as the means of combating God's hiddenness.[13] Thus, attempts to clarify or explain the actions of the hidden God other than the primary discourse of the gospel are to be confronted, because evading the gravity of God's hiddenness creates the potential for false hope. When it comes to God's hiddenness, those utilizing a Lutheran apologetic know when to keep silent and when to encourage others to do the same.

A Lutheran apologetic for the problem of evil and divine hiddenness is itself limited also, because apart from Christ, it cannot resolve the problem of evil and divine hiddenness definitively. This limited ability is not a weakness, as Mattes explains:

> Here's where apologetics can be handy. Sometimes you cannot prove something beyond a shadow of a doubt, but you can show that the opposing position is empty. That might be the only kind of proof which can be afforded in such matters. If your opponent's viewpoints are shown to be inconsistent or unsatisfactory, even though

11. Montgomery, "Defending the Hope," 11.

12. Luther, *Luther's Works*, 16:233–35.

13. Luther, *Luther's Works*, 5:43–50.

you have not proved your position, it is still the one left standing.[14]

The emptiness of the theological arguments denying God's hiddenness beyond wrath against human lawlessness, philosophical arguments denying God's existence, and theodicy models explaining God's actions is demonstrated when, despite the efforts of theologians and philosophers employing these methods, the hidden God remains lawless and unreasonable and his actions are often meaningless. "The pain of God cannot be removed by theological doctoring," writes Forde.[15] Consequently, Lutherans, at their best, remain mindful of the boundary and speak appropriately.

A Lutheran apologetic for the problem of evil and divine hiddenness is best described as a "negative apologetic" that consists of a clarifying component and a refutation component. The clarifying component is used to correct misunderstandings that people may have about Christianity, while the refutation component is used to counter false arguments attacking the faith. This latter component is becoming increasingly more necessary, because "chatterboxes," as Augustine called them, are vocal as ever, utilizing a host of formats to spread their message.[16] Employing all the appropriate apologetic tools available, the Lutheran apologist can, in fact, clarify the faith and refute the false claims of those attacking the faith. Still, a Lutheran apologetic will always be secondary discourse, especially when it comes to the problem of evil and divine hiddenness. No attempt should be made to remove or soften the mystery of God's hiding. Instead, "we have only God's awful hiddenness that cannot be separated, especially while it is underway, from evil itself."[17] Ultimately, the suffering created by the actions of the hidden God produces pastoral concerns that cannot be dealt with satisfactorily by theological and philosophical argumentation, hence the primacy of proclamation.

14. Mattes, "Lutheran Case for Apologetics," 28.

15. Forde, *Captivation of the Will*, 34.

16. Augustine, *Confessions*, bk. 1, 41.

17. Paulson, *Luther's Outlaw God*, 1:203.

A Sketch of a Lutheran Apologetic for the Problem of Evil and Divine Hiddenness

In the following, I will utilize the functions of a Lutheran apologetic established above to treat the most common elements of any discussion about the problem of evil and divine hiddenness. Included is consideration of evil's source, or origin; what evil is exactly, or evil's substance; how God's will relates to evil; and evil's longevity. Other facets of the discussion certainly exist. Evil's avoidance, theories of God's relationship to evil, and discussion of evil from polytheistic, pantheistic, and panentheistic perspectives are a few examples. Aspects such as these, though important and interesting, lay beyond the scope of this work.

The Origin of Evil

A seemingly perennial question concerns the origin of evil. The Scriptures are abundantly clear that the creation is good, so the question of evil's source quite naturally arises. Did God create evil? In that case, God is said to be evil. Is evil an inherent part of creation? If so, a kind of softness in God's omnipotence appears, if one assumes that a benevolent God would prevent the suffering evil produces. The majority of Christian thinkers have been reluctant to call God evil. Much more prevalent is the willingness to relax the insistence that God is omnipotent to make room for humans to be the origin of evil. Forced to balance God's sovereignty with evil's presence in creation, scholars argue correctly that creation is good, but they also assume God provides free choice for humanity. Consequently, evil's origin stems from humanity's failure to choose properly. In other words, God created a world with the potential for evil, but humanity, not God, is the cause. But, as we saw in the discussion about free-will theodicy, thinking in this manner simply introduces a regress back to the Creator. Either directly or indirectly, the result is the same. God is the source of evil, and how is simply a matter of taste.

At first glance, it would appear that Luther is in agreement with the vast majority of thinkers. He does, in fact, locate the human heart as the source of evil (Mark 7:15). Furthermore, as we saw earlier in the Heidelberg Disputation, he speaks of humanity possessing free will prior to the fall. Yet, in his debate with Erasmus, Luther modified his view, asserting throughout *The Bondage of the Will* that free will is an attribute of God, who alone possesses it.[18] This change is important, because it demonstrates Luther's reluctance to speculate about the hidden God. By maintaining God's immutable sovereignty while at the same time locating evil's source in the human heart, Luther refused to let God off the hook for evil. Luther's thought is limited and offers no reconciliation between God's sovereignty and human responsibility, demonstrating that the discussion is about God's hiddenness. Recognizing the lack of explanatory power that results from his assertion and no doubt aware of the potential regress his theological move creates, Luther is content nevertheless to stop the conversation with what is known from Scripture. Knowing the futility of attempting to figure God out apart from his words, Luther's thought also limits the certainty of explanations originating outside God's word, hence Luther's silence. He simply isn't interested in speculating about evil's origins beyond Jesus's words.

We do well to follow Luther's lead here. Fully aware of the questions that abound, the only certainty is that we don't know how God can rule all things immutably yet not be the source of evil. God is hidden deeply in this dilemma, and, as we've seen, assertions claiming to solve the quandary say too much. Law, reason, and rationales do not untie this theological knot, in spite of claims to the contrary. Furthermore, what good would result from knowing the origin of evil? Looking back solves nothing, because God is still to blame either as evil's source or for creating people with the propensity for evil. Paul's simile of the pot's protest to the potter, questioning the manner in which it was made, comes to mind (Rom 9:20–21). All that results from a search for evil's origin

18. Luther, *Luther's Works*, 33:103.

is Luther's "repugnant thought" that God is righteous and just no matter what. He writes:

> Admittedly, it gives the greatest possible offense to common sense or natural reason that God by his own sheer will should abandon, harden, and damn men as if he enjoyed the sins and the vast eternal torments of his wretched creatures, when he is preached as a God of such great mercy and goodness, etc. It has been regarded as unjust, as cruel, as intolerable, to entertain such an idea about God . . . And who would not be offended?[19]

Additionally, looking back undercuts proclamation by seeking to justify both God and humanity apart from God's words in the gospel. If God is responsible for evil, then humans shouldn't be to blame. If humans are responsible, then they are in some measure capable of mitigating the suffering caused by evil and theoretically capable of eradicating it. Whether adherence to law, denying or defending God's existence rationally, or explaining God's actions through theodicy, people have a role to play in taming evil and unmasking the hidden God.

Resurrecting people as active subjects capable of mitigating evil in some form or fashion seems to be the default position of those concerned with these matters. A review of the literature about the problem of evil and divine hiddenness puts this bondage to confidence in the human will on full display. Yet, assurance in human ability comes at the expense of proclamation, bypassing the fact that God's actions are justified by humanity and his benevolence revealed only in the preached gospel.

Speculation about evil's origin and human attempts to mitigate it are wholly beside the point. Recall that a Lutheran apologetic limits what those utilizing it can say. For that reason, pleading ignorance about the issue is better than risking the danger of undercutting the necessity of proclamation produced by speculative theological and philosophical constructs that typically rely on human ability.

---

19. Luther, *Luther's Works*, 33:190.

The Substance of Evil

Evil's substance, or nature, is another component of this discussion. Since God created all that exists, material and spiritual, the argument can be made that God created evil also. Augustine has done yeoman's work in defending God from the logic of such arguments. He maintains that evil is the absence of what is good in creation and is, therefore, parasitical in nature. As such, it is a nonentity and not created. Evil is the natural consequence of humans choosing to utilize creation in a manner not intended by God, like a hammer used as a weapon rather than used properly as a tool. Said another way, evil is the consequence of humanity behaving badly, not a creation of God. Yet, Augustine's argument does nothing to prevent the same regress found in the discussion of evil's origins, nor does his work unmask the hidden God's actions, establish his benevolence, and reduce human suffering.

Rather than speak of evil's substance abstractly, Luther defines evil as rebellious opposition stirred in the human heart by God's omnipotent will to work faith when and in whom he pleases. God hardening Pharaoh's heart illustrates human rebellion against his immutable will. God was determined to save the people of his choosing, and this election of Israel kindled violent opposition in Pharaoh. How the nature of Pharaoh's rebellion interacts with God's creation matters not to Luther. God's omnipotence produces rebellion, but Pharaoh is to blame.

The limited and limiting characteristics of Luther's thought are quite evident here. A simple glance at the news headlines seems to make Luther's talk of the substance of evil too narrow. In fact, philosophers of religion by and large, and many theologians, are reluctant to limit their reflection here and are broader than Luther in their thought. Marilyn McCord Adams, whom we briefly heard from earlier, provides an expansive description of evil's substance. She writes:

> It takes hard work to make planet Earth a hospitable place. Life's necessities seem to be in short supply. Food, water, shelter, and clothing are difficult to secure. Relative to the

hazards we encounter, our psycho-physical capacities are quite limited and easily damaged. At the biological level, we are vulnerable to predators, disease, and death. Coping with nature, eeking [*sic*] out survival, requires human collaboration, which brings its own problems. For we human beings do terrible things to one another, sometimes deliberately but also unintentionally, undeniably as individuals but certainly collectively, occasionally with carefully calibrated precision but often with unforeseen consequences that mushroom out of control.[20]

For Adams, the substance of evil is much more encompassing than rebellion against God for his election of people for salvation. All of life is marked by evil suffering, to say nothing of the "horrendous evils" that afflict some. Her description is true and superior to philosophical abstractions about the substance of evil, at least in a pastoral context.

My experience in the parish has been that suffering people aren't much interested in abstractions, like those of Augustine. Nor are they at a loss to explain the source of their suffering, which, in their mind at least, includes just about everything but rebellion against God's omnipotence. Thus, a broad understanding of evil's substance can serve as an entry point, leading ultimately to proclamation, in which rebellion is finally exposed and forgiven. Paulson illustrates this: "When we ourselves are in the middle of evil, talking about evil loses its fascination and conquering the evil is paramount."[21]

Though helpful in a pastoral context, expanding the description of evil's substance could go on indefinitely with very little accomplished. Worse, the potential for harm is introduced by this expansion if the thought is that evil can be "whittled down" so that each instance can be conquered by human effort in some form or fashion. We've seen this to be a common solution put forward by theologians and philosophers alike.

---

20. Adams, *Horrendous Evils*, 1.
21. Paulson, *Luther's Outlaw God*, 1:225.

Though cognizant of some pastoral benefit to an expanded understanding of evil's substance, a Lutheran apologetic is limited finally in its focus to what is certain—namely, rebellion against God's sovereignty as the substance of evil, remedied by proclamation only. This same focus limits those expanding evil's nature, thereby preventing the construction of human solutions. Evil's substance, the rebellion stirred by God's omnipotent election, is only alleviated when that election is proclaimed "for you."

God's Will and Evil

It is with more clarity that we can discuss this third component— God's will in relation to evil. Concluding that evil's presence is a manifestation of God's omnipotence, the opposite argument is that evil's presence means God is not omnipotent, or at least limited, and therefore unable to prevent evil. Neither option is particularly appealing to those wishing to maintain both God's sovereignty and his benevolence.

Thomas Aquinas offers a rather "hairsplitting" way forward here. He argues that God wills in two ways. God wills some things necessarily, leaving humanity no choice in the matter. God's existence is a prime example. Yet, God also wills some things conditionally, meaning that he has provided humanity with freedom and is willing to honor human choices. In other words, God's will, in some things, is not absolute but conditioned by human choices. Therefore, when humanity chooses badly, resulting in evil, humanity is to blame, not God.[22] In this second way of willing, Aquinas thinks to have made great strides in solving the problem of evil. Of course, Aquinas's argument is speculative, downplaying the testimony of God's messy omnipotence found in Scripture. Furthermore, his argument cannot escape the regress back to questions about the manner in which God created. Consequently, God's hiddenness is unmoved by Aquinas's sophistry.

---

22. Aquinas, *Summa Theologica*, 1.19.8–9.

Luther—and a Lutheran apologetic based on his thought—refuses to enter into Aquinas's speculative system. As we've seen throughout this work, treating divine hiddenness apart from the word of the gospel leads to the inescapable conclusion that in some fashion, evil and the suffering it produces are part of God's will. Consequently, a Lutheran apologetic insists that God's benevolent will is known only in the proclamation of the gospel. There, his omnipotence is revealed in the undeniable fact that when one is washed in the waters of baptism, is fed the bread and wine of the Lord's Supper, and hears the absolution given in the preached word, it is God's will of grace and mercy "for you." Because it happened, it is God's will!

Evil's Longevity

Evil's longevity is the last aspect of the problem of evil to be treated here. Given evil's persistence, either God's sovereignty or his benevolence appears questionable. It would appear that God cannot, or will not, put an end to evil and the consequent suffering it produces. The primacy of proclamation rises to the fore here also. Though true that in the death and resurrection of Christ, God has defeated evil, for the time being this fact is revealed only in the proclamation of the gospel promise, bringing to mind Luther's "light of glory" explained above.[23]

One quickly returns to God's hiddenness when seeking answers to the continued presence of evil. Speculation reigns supreme here, and no certain answers are forthcoming. Facing this dilemma without the benefit of the limiting function of a Lutheran apologetic, Jürgen Moltmann and other theologians, especially liberation theologians, have embarked on a program aimed at mitigating the effects of evil's longevity.[24] In brief, Moltmann argues

23. Luther, *Luther's Works*, 33:317.

24. See Lassalle-Klein, *Blood and Ink*. Lassalle-Klein provides an account of the Jesuits murdered at the University of Central America. A blood-soaked copy of Moltmann's book *The Crucified God* was found close to the body of Father Juan Moreno (Lassalle-Klein, *Blood and Ink*, xxii).

that being people of hope because of the gospel, Christians must not be content to allow evil to go unchallenged. The gospel creates in believers "a passion for the possible."[25] Therefore, as Christians work through appropriate means designed to alleviate evil and suffering, the eschatological promise of the gospel "breaks" into the present.

Moltmann's concern for the neighbor and the activity on behalf of the neighbor it has inspired is commendable, but his attempt to "put feet" to the gospel fails to diminish evil's persistence. Nevertheless, his theological program is highly influential for those stressing the importance of human ability to deal with evil. Yet, emphasizing the Christian's role in alleviating evil apart from proclamation is problematic. The truth is that we are forced to proclaim and then live by the promise of the gospel, waiting and suffering until the promise gives way to sight and evil's reality is extinguished, because we simply don't know why God allows evil to continue.

Summary

Our sketch of a Lutheran apologetic for the problem of evil and divine hiddenness looks like this. First, apart from the human heart as the source, the apologetic is silent about the ability to determine evil's origins conclusively. Second, the apologetic refuses to offer expansive definitions of evil's substance beyond rebellion against God's omnipotence. Third, the apologetic does not provide speculative statements about God's will in relation to evil's presence. Finally, the apologetic offers no rationale for evil's longevity. The apologetic, however, is not silent in its critique about the speculative nature of the arguments made by those claiming to know otherwise or the danger their claims pose to proclamation. The dogged insistence that God's benevolence remains staunchly hidden when sought apart from the gospel proclaimed is the contribution of an apologetic built on Luther's thought about the hidden

---

25. Moltmann, *Theology of Hope*, 35.

God, a fact captured by Forde, who writes, "The only solution to the problem of the absolute is actual absolution."[26]

The Canaanite Problem:
A Test Case for a Lutheran Apologetic

Given the unique contribution possible, Lutheran reluctance to enter the apologetic fray on the problem of evil and divine hiddenness is unfortunate. Arguments abound from apologists doing work in these areas without the insight offered by Luther's teaching. The results are often disastrous. One of the greatest examples is the apologetic treatment of the "Canaanite Problem."[27] In the following, some common apologetic arguments about the Canaanite Problem will be presented and critiqued using the apologetic distilled from Luther's thought.

Initial Considerations

> However, in the cities of the nations the LORD your God is giving you as an inheritance, do not leave alive anything that breathes. Completely destroy them—the Hittites, Amorites, the Canaanites, Perizzites, Hivites and Jebusites—as the LORD your God has commanded you. (Deut 20:16–17)

These are shocking words that offend believers and unbelievers alike. Worse, other troubling passages can be found throughout Scripture. Christians are left scrambling for answers, seemingly obliged to defend God from charges of immorality.[28]

---

26. Forde, *Preached God*, 152.

27. Richard Dawkins asserts that William Lane Craig locates God's benevolence in the death of the Canaanite children, who hadn't reached an "age of accountability" for sin. Thus, divinely commanded genocide ensured the children a place in the heavenly kingdom. See Dawkins, "Why I Refuse."

28. Copan, *Moral Monster*. Copan analyzes the ethical challenges presented by the "New Atheists."

Faced with the withering criticism, some Christian scholars have marshaled arguments designed to exonerate or at least mitigate the charges that God was immoral in his dealings with the inhabitants of the land. The first argument is the assumption that the people of the land possessed free will and therefore brought God's wrath upon themselves by their sinful choices. A second argument is that although God is merciful, he is also just and therefore required to visit wrath upon the evil people who were apparently beyond all hope. A third argument is that Near Eastern rhetoric in general, and the Hebrew language in particular, is nuanced and cannot necessarily be taken at face value.[29]

Feasting on Their Comeuppance: The Fruit of Free Will

Some scholars argue that the destruction of the people who inhabited the land of Canaan was the result of their bad choices. Speaking specifically about Jericho, the God of the Israelites was well known there. Rahab even says so: "We have heard how the LORD dried up the water of the Red Sea for you when you came out of Egypt . . . When we heard of it, our hearts melted and everyone's courage failed because of you, for the LORD your God is God in heaven above and on earth below" (Josh 2:10–11). The implication is that if Rahab, the prostitute, chose to believe, then everybody else could have believed. Furthermore, by marching around the city seven times, the inhabitants had additional time to believe. Consequently, God cannot be immoral for honoring the free will of the people. Their rejection of God led to their destruction.

An appeal to human free will to exonerate God is fallacious, because it fails to observe the guidelines of a Lutheran apologetic. A preliminary observation is that two elements are missing from the discussion. The first issue is that the discussion is rooted in the assumption that free will exists when, in fact, the human will is in bondage and will not choose to trust God apart from the work of the Holy Spirit giving faith. The second is a failure to note that God

29. Copan, *Moral Monster*, 158–97.

elects people for salvation through proclamation, giving mercy and grace to those whom he chooses. God's grace and mercy are a gift and not obtained by human choice. Therefore, the matter is about God's sovereignty, not the failure of the inhabitants of the land to exercise free will properly. Consequently, the argument does not address the hiddenness of God.

The argument does violate the guidelines distilled from Luther's thought. By ignoring the Scripture's teaching about God not preached, the text is twisted into a narrative that defends God by offering reasonable explanations for God's actions. Consequently, the fallacy of a magisterial use of reason arises. Furthermore, the argument violates the limiting function of a Lutheran apologetic by attempting to justify God apart from the word of the gospel. Finally, like all theodicies, the argument downplays the necessity of proclamation.

Rotten to the Core:
The Evilness of the People and the Justice of God

That the Canaanites were evil is beyond dispute. Sexual immorality was rampant in the culture and included both hetero- and homosexual acts in religious temples. Bestiality, incest, and child sacrifice were common also. The Scriptures even speak of the wickedness of the nations as the cause of their judgment (Deut 9:4–5). The argument is made that God is a God of justice and cannot allow evil to continue unabated. Thus, he cannot be immoral for punishing the people's wickedness. Their evil practices led to their destruction.

Exonerating God by appeals to his justice and obligation to punish evil are more convincing. Both elements are true, and in that sense, the inhabitants of the land got what they deserved. Still, an element of capriciousness is present. Some cities were to be offered peace treaties (Deut 20:10–11). Not so for "the cities of the nations" that God was giving to the Israelites (Deut 20:16). The reason given for their utter destruction is the spiritual protection of the Israelites (Deut 20:18). Granted, punishment for evil is implied, but the text is not specific about that motivation. Furthermore, God's command also indicates that the Israelites were just as capable of evil as the inhabitants of the land, a fact confirmed in other parts of Scripture when the Israelites committed the same evil actions.

Other than the presence of the Israelites, why did God destroy just the inhabitants of the land at that particular time? An argument can be made from Scripture that the fullness of their evil had finally arrived (Deut 9:4–5). However, for the Israelite slaves in the mud pits of Egypt, allowing the evilness of the Canaanites to determine God's timing raises questions about his benevolence. Furthermore, is one to conclude that the Exodus was dependent upon the Canaanites? That move is similar to that of those who dispute the text concerning God actively hardening Pharaoh's heart. By treating that passage as a trope, the timing of the Exodus becomes dependent upon Pharaoh. Treating the text in this manner is backward, and arguments fashioned in this manner say too much in an effort to exonerate God. The fact is that God chose the time and the recipients of his destruction because of his immutable will seen in the election of Israel, not simply to punish evil. Once again, the hiddenness of God is at work, not the actions of humanity. Therefore, the question of God's lawfulness in dealing with the inhabitants of the land remains open, thereby highlighting the necessity of utilizing the limiting function of a Lutheran apologetic.

Can the Text be Trusted?

Was the utter destruction of Jericho literal? Copan and others think not, prompting Copan to assert that "the conquest of Canaan was far less widespread and harsh than many people assume."[30] He and other scholars describe the conquest accounts as "ancient Near Eastern exaggeration rhetoric."[31] Based on settlement accounts

---

30. Copan, *Moral Monster*, 170.

31. Copan, *Moral Monster*, 170–72.

in Judges that speak of the gradual assimilation of the Israelites throughout the land, scholars conclude that Joshua was using a grandiose writing style common during that time. Additionally, some Old Testament scholars argue that the Hebrew word *herem*, which means "ban" or "consecration to destruction," should not be understood to include noncombatants. The implication is that the destruction of the people of the land was more strategic and less comprehensive than typically thought. Thus, God is not immoral, because his divine commands to the Israelites did not call for utter destruction.

Attempts to exonerate God using textual arguments are weak. The Scripture is clear about God's treatment of the land's inhabitants, especially the city of Jericho. "They devoted the city to the LORD and destroyed with the sword every living thing in it— men and women, young and old, cattle, sheep, and donkeys" (Josh 6:21). Furthermore, and in spite of Kathleen Kenyon's claims,[32] archeological evidence does seem to exist that Jericho was destroyed in a manner consistent with the biblical account.[33] Claiming that Joshua was simply bragging or that Hebrew words may not mean what the text says they mean is fraught with difficulty. The authority of Scripture guards against such arguments, leading to the conclusion that God has not asked to be defended outside his word of gospel, nor can he be.

In sum, I find arguments attempting to exonerate God from moral culpability unconvincing. God is sovereign, a fact pointed out by Paul Moser, who writes:

> It would be a strange, defective God who didn't pose a serious cosmic authority problem for humans. Part of the status of being God, after all, is that God has a unique authority, or lordship over humans. Since we humans

---

32. Archaeologist Kathleen Kenyon cast doubt on the factualness of the biblical account of Jericho's fall. See Holden and Geisler, *Popular Handbook*, 183.

33. Holden and Geisler, *Popular Handbook*, 235–38.

aren't God, the true God would have authority over us
and would seek to correct our profoundly selfish ways.[34]

God, not humans, was in control of the timing and the rationale for his treatment of the inhabitants of the land. Furthermore, God seeks no justification from humans for the manner in which he dealt with the inhabitants, thereby illustrating the accuracy of Paul's argument in Romans. Therefore, attempts to defend God's treatment of the inhabitants of the land fail.

The failure of the arguments illustrates the advantage of an apologetic built on the insight of Luther's thought. By using reason as an organizational tool rather than a guiding standard and linking God's justification strictly to his word in the gospel instead of some standard of justice, speculation about God's hiddenness is avoided. The gospel of Jesus Christ proclaimed "for you" is put forward as the solution to the problem of evil and divine hiddenness.

34. Moser, "Death, and Meaning," 221–22.

Selected Bibliography

Adams, Marilyn McCord. *Horrendous Evils and the Goodness of God*. Ithaca, New York: Cornell University Press, 1999.

Adams, Robert M. "A Modified Divine Command Theory of Ethical Wrongness." In *Religion and Morality*, edited by Gene Outka and John P. Reeder, 318–47. Garden City, NY: Doubleday, 1973.

Althaus, Paul. *The Theology of Martin Luther*. Translated by Robert C. Schultz. Philadelphia: Fortress, 1966.

Augustine. *City of God*. Edited by Vernon J. Bourke. Translated by Gerald Walsh et al. Garden City, New York: Image, 1958.

———. *The Confessions*. Translated by Maria Boulding. Edited by John E. Rotelle. Hyde Park, NY: New City, 1997.

Aquinas, Thomas. *Summa Theologica*. Claremont, CA: Coyote Canyon, 2018.

Barnett, S. J. "Where Was Your Church before Luther? Claims for the Antiquity of Protestantism Examined." *Church History* 68.1 (March 1999) 14–41.

Barth, Hans-Martin. *The Theology of Martin Luther: A Critical Assessment*. Minneapolis: Fortress, 2013.

Bayer, Oswald. "God's Omnipotence." Translated by Jonathan Mumme. *Lutheran Quarterly* 23.1 (Spring 2009) 85–102.

———. *Martin Luther's Theology: A Contemporary Interpretation*. Translated by Thomas H. Trapp. Grand Rapids: Eerdmans, 2008.

———. *Theology the Lutheran Way*. Edited and translated by Jeffrey G. Silcock and Mark C. Mattes. Grand Rapids: Eerdmans, 2007.

Becker, Siegbert. *The Foolishness of God: The Place of Reason in the Theology of Martin Luther*. Milwaukee: Northwestern, 2009.

Brenton, Lancelot Charles Lee. *The Septuagint with Apocrypha: Greek and English*. Peabody, MA: Hendrickson, 1986.

Chalmers, A F. *What Is This Thing Called Science?* 4th ed. Indianapolis: Hackett, 2013.

Chesterton, G. K. *Orthodoxy*. San Francisco: Ignatius, 1995.

Childs, Brevard S. *Biblical Theology of the Old and New Testaments: Theological Reflection on the Christian Bible*. Minneapolis: Fortress, 1993.

Clifford, Richard J. *Abingdon Old Testament Commentaries, Psalms 1–72.* Nashville: Abingdon, 2002.

Cobb, John, Jr., and David Ray Griffin. *Process Theology: An Introductory Exposition.* Philadelphia: Westminster, 1976.

Copan, Paul. *Is God a Moral Monster? Making Sense of the Old Testament God.* Grand Rapids: Baker, 2011.

Craig, William Lane. *On Guard: Defending Your Faith with Reason and Precision.* Colorado Springs, CO: David C. Cook, 2010.

————. *Reasonable Faith: Christian Truth and Apologetics.* 3rd ed. Wheaton, IL: Crossway, 2008.

Crossan, John Dominic. *Jesus: A Revolutionary Biography.* New York: Harper Collins, 1991.

Darwin, Charles. *On the Origin of Species by Means of Natural Selection.* Oxford: Oxford University Press, 1872.

Davis, Stephen T. *Encountering Evil: Live Options in Theodicy.* Louisville: Westminster John Knox, 2001.

Dawkins, Richard. *The God Delusion.* Boston: Houghton Mifflin, 2006.

————. "Why I Refuse to Debate with William Lane Craig." *Guardian,* October 20, 2011. https://www.theguardian.com/commentisfree/2011/oct/20/richard-dawkins-william-lane-craig.

Dennett, Daniel. *Breaking the Spell: Religion as a Natural Phenomenon.* New York: Penguin, 2007.

Dillenberger, John. *God Hidden and Revealed: The Interpretation of Luther's Deus Absconditus and Its Significance for Religious Thought.* Philadelphia: Muhlenberg, 1953.

Draper, Paul. "Arguments from Evil." In *Philosophy of Religion: Classic and Contemporary Issues,* edited by Paul Copan and Chad. V. Meister, 142–55. Oxford: Blackwell, 2008.

Ebeling, Gerhard. *God and Word.* Translated by James W. Leitch. Philadelphia: Fortress, 1967.

————. *Luther: An Introduction to His Thought.* Translated by R. A. Wilson. Philadelphia: Fortress, 2007.

Ehrman, Bart. *God's Problem: How the Bible Fails to Answer Our Most Important Question—Why We Suffer.* New York: HarperCollins, 2008.

Elert, Werner. *The Structure of Lutheranism.* Vol. 1, *The Theology and Philosophy of Life of Lutheranism, Especially in the Sixteenth and Seventeenth Centuries,* translated by Walter A. Hansen. Saint Louis: Concordia, 1962.

Ennis, Garth. *Preacher.* New York: Vertigo, 1995.

Feinberg, John S. *The Many Faces of Evil: Theological Systems and the Problem of Evil.* Wheaton, IL: Crossway, 2004.

Forde, Gerhard O. *The Captivation of the Will: Luther vs. Erasmus on Freedom and Bondage.* Edited by Steven D. Paulson. Grand Rapids: Eerdmans, 2005.

————. *The Essential Forde: Distinguishing Law and Gospel.* Edited by Nicholas Hopman et al. Minneapolis: Fortress, 2019.

————. *On Being a Theologian of the Cross: Reflections on Luther's Heidelberg Disputation*. Grand Rapids: Eerdmans, 1997.

————. *The Preached God: Proclamation in Word and Sacrament*. Edited by Mark Mattes and Steven Paulson. Grand Rapids: Eerdmans, 2007.

————. "Radical Lutheranism." *Lutheran Quarterly* 1 (1987) 1–16.

————. *Theology Is for Proclamation*. Minneapolis: Fortress, 1990.

————. *Where God Meets Man: Luther's Down-to-Earth Approach to the Gospel*. Minneapolis: Augsburg, 1972.

Francisco, Adam S., et al., eds. *Theologia et Apologia: Essays in Reformation Theology and Its Defense Presented to Rod Rosenblatt*. Eugene, OR: Wipf & Stock, 2007.

Gerhard, Johann. *Theological Commonplaces*. Vol. 1, *On the Nature of God and on the Trinity*. Edited by Benjamin T. G. Mayes. Translated by Richard J. Dinda. St. Louis: Concordia, 2007.

Gerrish, Brian A. "To the Unknown God: Luther and Calvin on the Hiddenness of God." *Journal of Religion* 53 (1973) 263–92.

"Glosses Reveal a Gnostic Luther." Unam Sanctam Catholicam. http://unamsanctamcatholicam.com/history/79-history/383-glosses-reveal-a-gnostic-luther.html.

Grenz, Stanley. *Pocket Dictionary of Theological Terms*. Downers Grove, IL: InterVarsity, 1999.

Eagleton, Terry. *Reason, Faith, and Revolution: Reflections on the God Debate*. New Haven, CT: Yale University Press, 2009.

Harris, Sam. *Letter to a Christian Nation*. New York: Random House, 2008.

Heschel, Abraham. *The Prophets*. New York: Harper & Row, 1962.

Hick, John. *Death and Eternal Life*. Louisville: Westminster John Knox, 1994.

————. *Evil and the God of Love*. New York: Palgrave Macmillan, 2007.

Hinson, Ed, and Ergun Caner, eds. *The Popular Encyclopedia of Apologetics: Surveying the Evidence for the Truth of Christianity*. Eugene, OR: Harvest House, 2008.

Hitchens, Christopher. *God Is Not Great: How Religion Poisons Everything*. New York: Twelve Hachette, 2007.

Holden, Joseph M., and H. Wayne House. *Charts of Apologetics and Christian Evidences*. Grand Rapids: Zondervan, 2006.

Holden, Joseph M., and Norman Geisler. *The Popular Handbook of Archaeology and the Bible*. Eugene, OR: Harvest House, 2013.

Holl, Karl. *What Did Luther Understand by Religion?* Edited by James Luther Adams and Walter F. Bense. Translated by Fred W. Meuser and Walter R. Wietzke. Philadelphia: Fortress, 1977.

Howard-Snyder, Daniel, and Michael Bergmann. "Evil Does Not Make Atheism More Reasonable than Theism." In *Contemporary Debates in Philosophy of Religion*, edited by Michael L. Peterson and Raymond J. Vanarragon, 13–25. Malden, MA: Blackwell, 2004.

Howard-Synder, Daniel, and Paul K. Moser, eds. *Divine Hiddenness: New Essays*. Cambridge: University Press, 2002.

Iwand, Hans J. *The Righteousness of Faith according to Luther*. Eugene, OR: Wipf & Stock , 2008.

Jüngel, Eberhard. *God as the Mystery of the World: On the Foundation of the Theology of the Crucified One in the Dispute between Theism and Atheism*. Translated by Darrell L. Gruder. Grand Rapids: Eerdmans, 1983.

King, Stephen. *Revival*. New York: Scribner, 2014.

Kolb, Robert. *Bound Choice, Election, and the Wittenberg Theological Method*. Grand Rapids: Eerdmans, 2005.

Kolb, Robert, and Timothy J. Wengert, eds. *The Book of Concord: The Confessions of the Evangelical Lutheran Church*. Minneapolis: Fortress, 2000.

Lassalle-Klein, Robert. *Blood and Ink: Ignacio Ellacuria, Jon Sobrino, and the Jesuit Martyrs of the University of Central America*. Maryknoll: Orbis, 2014.

Lawson, Steven J. *Holman Old Testament Commentary, Psalm 1–75*. Nashville: Broadman & Holman, 2003.

Lienhard, Marc. *Luther: Witness to Jesus Christ*. Translated by Edwin H. Robertson. Minneapolis: Augsburg, 1982.

Lohse, Bernhard. *Martin Luther's Theology: Its Historical and Systematic Development*. Translated by Roy A. Harrisville. Minneapolis: Fortress, 1999.

Luther, Martin. *The Bondage of the Will*. Translated by J. I. Packer and O. R. Johnston. Grand Rapids: Fleming H. Revell, 2006.

———. *Commentary on Romans*. Translated by J. Theodore Mueller. Grand Rapids: Kregel, 1993.

———. *A Compend of Luther's Theology*. Whitefish, MT: Kessinger, 2010.

———. *Luther's Works*. Edited by Jaroslav Pelikan and Helmut T. Lehmann. 55 vols. Philadelphia: Fortress, 1955–86.

Maas, Korey D., and Adam S. Francisco, eds. *Making the Case for Christianity: Responding to Modern Objections*. Saint Louis: Concordia, 2014.

Mackie, J. L. "Evil and Omnipotence." In *The Problem of Evil*, 2nd ed., edited by Michael L. Peterson, 81–94. Notre Dame, IN: University of Notre Dame Press, 2017.

Macquarrie, John, and James F. Childress, eds. *The Westminster Dictionary of Christian Ethics*. Philadelphia: Westminster, 1986.

Maher, Bill. *Religulous*. Directed by Larry Charles. 1 hr., 41 min. Thousand Words, 2008.

"Martin Luther." Reforming to Scripture. http://reformingtoscripture.com/resources/articles/history/martin-luther/.

Mattes, Mark C. "A Lutheran Case for Apologetics." *Logia* 24.3 (2015) 25–32.

———. *Martin Luther's Theology of Beauty: A Reappraisal*. Grand Rapids: Baker Academic, 2017.

———. *The Role of Justification in Contemporary Theology*. Grand Rapids: Eerdmans, 2004.

McGrath, Alister E. *Dawkins' God: From the Selfish Gene to the God Delusion*. 2nd ed. West Sussex, UK: Wiley Blackwell, 2015.

————. *Mere Apologetics: How to Help Seekers and Skeptics Find Faith.* Grand Rapids: Baker, 2012.

Meister, Chad, and James K. Dew Jr., eds. *God and the Problem of Evil: Five Views.* Downers Grove, IL: InterVarsity, 2017.

Meuser, Fred W. *Luther the Preacher.* Minneapolis: Augsburg, 1983.

Middendorf, Michael P. *Concordia Commentary, Romans 1–8.* Saint Louis: Concordia, 2013.

Miller, Joshua C. *Hanging by a Promise: The Hidden God in the Theology of Oswald Bayer.* Eugene, OR: Pickwick, 2015.

Moltmann, Jurgen. *Theology of Hope.* Minneapolis: Fortress, 1993.

Montgomery, John Warwick. *Christ as Centre and Circumference.* Eugene, OR: Wipf & Stock, 2012.

————. "Defending the Hope That Is in Us: Apologetics for the Twenty-First Century." Lecture. Hope for Europe Conference, Evangelical Alliance, Budapest, Hungary, 2002.

————. ed. *Evidence for Faith: Deciding the God Question.* Dallas: Probe, 1991.

————. *History, Law, and Christianity.* Irvine, CA: NRP, 2014.

————. *Tractatus Logico-Theologicus.* Eugene, OR: Wipf & Stock, 2013.

Moo, Douglas J. *The Epistle to the Romans.* New International Commentary on the New Testament. Grand Rapids: Eerdmans, 1996.

Morley, Brian K. *Mapping Apologetics: Comparing Contemporary Approaches.* Downers Grove, IL: InterVarsity, 2015.

Moser, Paul K. "Divine Hiddenness, Death, and Meaning." In *Philosophy of Religion: Classic and Contemporary Issues*, edited by Paul Copan and Chad Meister, 215–28. Oxford: Blackwell, 2008.

————. "Divine Hiddenness Does Not Justify Atheism." In *Contemporary Debates in Philosophy of Religion*, edited by Michael L. Peterson and Raymond J. Vanarragon, 42–54. Malden, MA: Blackwell, 2004.

Nestingen, James A. "Introduction: Luther and Eramus on the Bondage of the Will." In *The Captivation of the Will: Luther vs. Erasmus on Freedom and Bondage*, by Gerhard Forde, 1–21. Edited by Steven D. Paulson. Grand Rapids: William B. Eerdmans, 2005.

Ngien, Dennis. *Fruit for the Soul: Luther on the Lament Psalms.* Minneapolis: Fortress, 2015.

Otto, Rudolph. *The Idea of the Holy.* Translated by John W. Harvey. London: Oxford University Press, 1958.

Paulson, Steven D. *Luther for Armchair Theologians.* Louisville: Westminster John Knox, 2004.

————. "Luther on the Hidden God." *Word and World* 19.4 (Fall 1999) 363–71.

————. *Luther's Outlaw God.* 3 vols. Minneapolis: Fortress, 2018–21.

————. *Lutheran Theology.* London: Bloomsbury, 2011.

Peterson, Michael L., ed. *The Problem of Evil.* 2nd ed. Notre Dame, IN: University of Notre Dame Press, 2017.

Peterson, Michael L., and Raymond J. Vanarragon, eds. *Contemporary Debates in Philosophy of Religion.* Malden, MA: Blackwell, 2004.

Pinnock, Clark H. *Most Moved Mover: A Theology of God's Openness.* Grand Rapids: Baker, 2001.

Placher, William C. *The Domestication of Transcendence: How Modern Theology about God Went Wrong.* Louisville: Westminster John Knox, 1996.

Plantinga, Alvin. *God, Freedom, and Evil.* Grand Rapids: Eerdmans, 1977.

Rad, Gerhard von. *Old Testament Theology.* Vol. 1. New York: Harper & Row, 1962.

Rea, Michael C. *The Hiddenness of God.* Oxford: Oxford University Press, 2018.

Rosenbladt, Rod. *Christ Alone.* Wheaton, IL: Crossway, 1999.

Rowe, William L. "Evil Is Evidence against Theistic Belief." In *Contemporary Debates in Philosophy of Religion,* edited by Michael L. Peterson and Raymond J. Vanarragon, 3–13. Malden, MA: Blackwell, 2004.

———. *Philosophy of Religion: An Introduction.* Belmont, CA: Wadsworth Cengage Learning, 2007.

Schellenberg, J. L. "Divine Hiddenness Justifies Atheism." In *Contemporary Debates in Philosophy of Religion,* edited by Michael L. Peterson and Raymond J. Vanarragon, 30–41. Malden, MA: Blackwell, 2004.

———. *The Hiddenness Argument: Philosophy's New Challenge to Belief in God.* Oxford: Oxford University Press, 2015.

Schlink, Edmund. *The Doctrine of Baptism.* Translated by Herbert J. A. Bouman. Saint Louis: Concordia, 1972.

Scott, Mark S. M. *Pathways in Theodicy: An Introduction to the Problem of Evil.* Minneapolis: Fortress, 2015.

Seifrid, Mark A. "Righteousness, Justice, Justification." In *New Dictionary of Biblical Theology,* edited by T. Desmond Alexander et al., 740–45. Downers Grove, IL: InterVarsity, 2000.

Smith, Ralph L. *Old Testament Theology: Its History, Method, and Message.* Nashville: Broadman & Holman, 1993.

Stein, James K. "Philip Jakob Spener." In *The Pietist Theologians: An Introduction to Theology in the Seventeenth and Eighteenth Centuries,* edited by Carter Lindberg, 84–99. Oxford: Blackwell, 2005.

Steinmetz, David C. *Luther in Context.* 2nd ed. Grand Rapids: Baker Academic, 2002.

Tate, Marvin. *Word Biblical Commentary.* Vol. 20, *Psalms 51–100.* Grand Rapids: Zondervan, 1991.

Weiss, James Michael. "Erasmus at Luther's Funeral: Melanchthon's Commemorations of Luther in 1546." *Sixteenth Century Journal* 16.1 (Spring 1985) 91–114.

Whybray, R. N. *Isaiah 40-66.* The New Century Bible Commentary. Edited by Ronald Clements and Matthew Black. Grand Rapids: Eerdmans, 1981.

Widengren Geo. *Mani and Manichaeism.* Translated by Charles Kessler. New York: Holt, Rinehart & Winston, 1965.

Wolterstorff, Nicholas. *Lament for a Son.* Grand Rapids: Eerdmans, 1987.

————. "The Silence of the God Who Speaks." In *Divine Hiddenness: New Essays*, edited by Daniel Howard-Synder and Paul K. Moser, 215–28. Cambridge: Cambridge Unversity Press, 2002.

Žižek, Slavoj, and Boris Gunjević. *God in Pain: Inversions of Apocalypse.* New York: Seven Stories, 2012.

CPSIA information can be obtained
at www.ICGtesting.com
Printed in the USA
LVHW082133251022
731586LV00029B/970

9 781666 718492